(Inner) FITness™ and The FIT Corporation™

Living and working in the present tense

(Inner) FITness™ and The FIT Corporation™

Living and working in the present tense

Ben (C) Fletcher and Bob Stead

THOMSON

★
™

LEARNING   Australia • Canada • Mexico • Singapore • Spain • United Kingdom • United States

(Inner) FITness™ and The FIT Corporation™

Copyright © 2000 Ben (C) Fletcher and Bob Stead

(Inner) FITness, The FIT Profiler, The FIT Corporation are trademarks claimed by The FIT Corporation Ltd, University of Hertfordshire, AL10 9AB, UK.

Thomson Learning™ is a trademark used herein under licence.

For more information, contact Thomson Learning, Berkshire House, 168–173 High Holborn, London, WC1V 7AA or visit us on the World Wide Web at: http://www.thomsonlearning.co.uk

British Library Cataloguing-in-Publication Data
A catalogue record for this book is available from the British Library

ISBN 1-86152-644-X

First edition published 2000 by Thomson Learning

Typeset by LaserScript Limited, Mitcham, Surrey
Printed in the UK by TJ International, Padstow, Cornwall
Cover design by Words and Pictures

for Nellie
thanks for inspiration Elio and Stefano

Contents

Preface

In an interview before he died the British playwright Dennis Potter was discussing what he felt was important to do in life that he had learned from having a terminal disease that was soon to kill him. He said he tried to live every moment and experience in the present tense. That gave every sense and experience an intensity, freshness and reality that it would not otherwise have. He did not know about FIT theory, but *(Inner) FITness*™ is also about living in the present tense, instead of in the past tense as so many do.

Despite what they believe to be the case, people do not generally choose what to do, decide or think: they are victims of their past and their organic and psychological building blocks. Like it or not, past behaviours predict future behaviours and (what you call) intentions do little to intervene. Intentions are themselves deceitful. We believe we humans will them (after all, to intend is to be human) but we would do well to realize that intentions are largely formed by past behaviours. We are animals after all. FITness is about trying to be human and EXERcising choice and real change. It is about taking control of the 'now' and designing the future, instead of allowing the future simply to be the past continued.

CHAPTER ONE

The principles of (Inner) FITness™

The skeleton or basic principles of *(Inner) FITness*™ are laid bare in the following statements with only the supporting evidence of your own intuitions. Evidence comes in later chapters, although we also offer some suggestions about what status 'scientific evidence' should have – different criteria might be more rigorous and useful, such as the propensity to act as springs of action, or the relevance to people's lives. We have deliberately chosen a positive and definite style to portray the core aspects of FITness in order to incite thought and counter-claim. The FIT framework is a simple one. We believe in the power of simplicity even if there is some cost (primarily psychological, in our view) to not having layers of complexity to obfuscate clarity. Most important issues are simple and more complicated answers relevant to less important questions. The (Inner) FITness™ theory is a broad one but does not encompass all possibilities.

Like all important or interesting aspects in life, FIT theory requires a leap of faith. FITness is at that edge. The leap is no bigger than the ones you already take, or have taken (but often do not realize). It might be more apposite to say it requires a forward-looking and open mind. If you are challenged, that is good. If the statements make you think, that is good. If you can see the value of *(Inner) FITness*™, you will share some of our views: these parts of our worlds overlap too. What is put in words here is not quickly penned to satisfy an editor or you. The words are written with our own *Integrity* for guidance, but not an Integrity that is at stake. We believe in their value. If you reject what is here without thought then you should examine yourself – not because you are rejecting the words we have carefully chosen, but because your clarity of mind suggests a habitual prejudice. That accusation should have new meaning after you have read the statements. None of us have really open minds, but we should not be bound by personal frameworks that are narrow enough to blot out all but what we clearly believe now: that does not show maturity or growth potential, but deep freezing.

You will discover that some words do not mean what you might expect them to mean. We have robbed them for our own pleasure. These are indicated by the use of capital letters where they would not normally be. 'FITness' is one of these. We have even taken some deliberate liberties with the English language. No doubt there are many non-deliberate misuses too.

The Statements

0.0   Many people are unhappy, unhealthy or unsuccessful.
0.1   According to *(Inner) FITness*™ this is due to a number of principal *locks*:
0.1.1   For most people, *fear*, and its family, is a major determinant of decision and action,
0.1.2   Many believe that they are bound by external *chains* and constraints,
0.1.3   People are *unaware* and inattentive, or sleep with their eyes open, and let it happen,
0.1.4   The various important parts of life are out of *balance*,
0.1.5   Need for *external* success is a primary goal.

0.2   People have the freedom to choose to be constrained or not.
0.2.1   Most people choose constraint and build a world upon it.
0.2.2   It can be different, and you can make it so, whatever you think.

0.3   The most deterministic aspect of your universe is due to your own choices. It is that inevitability that can alter. By you making active choices.

1.0   The key to health, happiness and success is *(Inner) FITness*™.
1.0.1   That is all that is required.

1.1   *FITness* involves a present and future perspective, rather than a past one.
1.1.1   *(Inner) FITness*™ promotes living in the present tense, not the past tense.

1.1.2   The past contains too much of the future for the *unFIT* (and the future too much of the past).

1.1.3   FITness requires the individual to use their learning to help cement future decisions, not to shape them.

1.1.3.1   There is a crucial difference between learning from experience and passively having the experience: FIT people learn and have, unFIT just have.

1.2   ((Inner)) FITness is a worthy goal for anyone.

1.2.1   *(Inner) FITness™* benefits everyone.

1.3   All can be FITter with practice, but most become more unFIT with their practices.

2.0   Fitness is an aid to bodily health and *(Inner) FITness™* to mental health.

2.0.1   Mental health is not dependent upon *(Inner) FITness™*, but FITness precludes poor mental well-being.

2.1   *(Inner) FITness™* aids physical fitness, and fitness aids FITness.

2.1.1   *Total FITness* is synonymous with *(Inner) FITness™*, or to put this another way, FITness is superior to fitness in its benefits.

3.0   *(Inner) FITness™* means always acting with FIT *Integrity*.

3.0.1   FITness involves regaining personal integration – or one's core self – from the centrifugal forces that act to disintegrate it.

3.0.1.1   These disintegrating forces, which chart the topography of the FIT Killing Fields, are in the past and include personal history and past learning; social pressures; genes; parental pressures; environmental demands, including work demands; and other 'outer needs'.

3.1   FIT Integrity is a wholesome and deep property.

3.1.1   FIT Integrity makes itself manifest without words.

3.2   The person who acts with Integrity will be charismatic as well as internally strong.

3.2.1   Many people think they act with Integrity, but most do not.

3.2.2   Anyone who thinks they are FIT, or that they act with Integrity, is not and does not.

3.3	Success has an external and an internal dimension.
3.3.1	Success is often confused with something else that has only an external dimension.
3.4	*(Inner) FITness™* is always apparent to others for its value and power.
3.4.1	Some people are threatened by value and power in others.
3.5	No other personal qualities can successfully compete with that involved in the (Inner) FITness framework.
3.5.1	A FIT person will always succeed against an unFIT one in the long term.
3.5.2	The FIT person does not compete, but wins.
3.6	Winning is easy, but not without effort.
3.6.1	Effort is needed to decide and behave according to the *Five Constancies.*
3.6.1.1	The Constancies provide the Growing Fields for the individual.
3.6.1.2	The Constancies can provide the scaffolding for our model of the world.
4.0	The Five Constancies are *Awareness, Fearlessness, Self-responsibility, Morality and Ethics,* and *Balance.*
4.0.1	Deciding and behaving according to the Constancies is Integrity.
4.0.2	The Constancies provide the centripetal integrating forces against the Killing Fields of past disintegration.
4.1	*Awareness* is the engine of FITness.
4.1.1	Awareness is being awake to all relevant information provided to the mind and the senses.
4.1.1.1	Another word to describe awareness would be attentiveness.
4.1.1.2	The degree of awareness is the extent to which a person monitors and attends to their external and internal worlds.
4.1.2	Awareness is more than being awake.
4.1.3	Most people are not aware of most things most of the time. Most could be described as being asleep with their eyes open.
4.1.4	An aware person has much more information at his or her disposal than does someone who sleeps.
4.1.5	Awareness expands time.

4.1.5.1   Total awareness expands time totally.

4.1.5.2   The person who is aware has all the time in the world at that time.

4.1.5.3   Time flies for older people because they have more habits to stop them paying attention.

4.1.6   FIT people can utilize time, not be contained by it, because of their level of awareness.

4.1.7   There are different levels of awareness and different levels of things to be aware of.

4.1.7.1   Total awareness encapsulates all these levels.

4.1.8   The FIT cannot be aware of everything relevant to the now. Some call that God's role. But the FIT are gods of their own world because that is everything they are aware of.

4.2   *Self-responsibility* involves taking charge of your life and acting as though you can determine what will happen.

4.2.1   The degree of self-responsibility is the extent to which a person accepts personal accountability for their world irrespective of factors outside themselves.

4.2.2   Those who ascribe to FITness take it as axiomatic that the world shapes itself around the individual. Thoughts become concrete and turn ideas to reality.

4.2.3   A person's world reflects their shaping of it.

4.2.3.1   This is true of the worlds of the FIT and the unFIT.

4.2.4   To shape something, it is better to have well-heeded thoughts about what shape one wants to create.

4.2.5   The FIT must look after themselves. The unFIT do not (and cannot).

4.2.6   'They' play a major part in the lives of the unFIT.

4.3   Self-responsible people see that random factors are simply those that have not been heeded, or, to put it another way, those that the person has not taken responsibility for.

4.3.1   A person can only have what they can take responsibility for.

4.3.2   Taking responsibility for something means more than desiring and fantasizing about it.

4.3.2.1   To take responsibility means to attend to it properly.

4.3.3   Luck is a failure to take heed of, or to account for, all relevant factors. It is what is left as explanation for the unFIT.

4.3.4   FIT people are not lucky, although they appear lucky to the unFIT.

4.3.5   In FITness nothing is accidental: accidents do not happen to the FIT.

4.4   *Balance* is when each aspect of life receives due care and attention.

4.4.1   Balance requires that the important areas of a person's life should have appropriate focus, that sufficient effort be put into them and that they should receive sufficient satisfaction from them.

4.4.2   A person who achieves balance makes each area, or part, work positively for the others. The areas and parts should be positively synergistic.

4.4.3   Without balance there is antagonism between the various areas.

4.4.4   For many people there are at least three areas to balance: Work (the labour dimension); Non-work (the social dimension); and the Self-dimension.

4.4.4.1   Each area is also composed of parts, which also require balancing.

4.5   *Morality and ethics* is differentiating between what is right and what is wrong and doing what is right.

4.5.1   Morality is a personal absolute, and is not defined by others.

4.5.2   The moral person is virtuous when they act in accordance with the other Constancies.

4.5.2.1   Otherwise they are merely extolling virtues.

4.5.3   The person who acts with Integrity acts morally.

4.5.3.1   That morality is common to all.

4.6   *Fearlessness* is acting without fear or trepidation.

4.6.1   Fear is not always explicit, but decisions and behaviours are often done through implicit or past-induced fear.

4.6.2   Fear is the cause of unhappiness as well as cognitive thought restriction.

4.6.2.1   Fearful people are less adventurous and may make fewer mistakes.

4.6.2.2   Fearful people are critical of the mistakes of others out of jealousy.

4.6.3   Fearless people can have emotional intelligence.

5.0   Constancy levels cannot be too high for the FIT.

5.0.1   For the unFIT Constancy levels may not be in harmony.

5.0.2   Harmony produces harmonics, lack of harmony, discord.

5.1   Harmony between the Constancies is better than relatively too much strength in some.

5.1.1   Lack of harmony between the Constancies, and imbalance between them in terms of their strength or weakness, causes multifarious problems.

5.1.1.1   Too much fear causes illness, but fearlessness unchained from the other Constancies, stupidity and brazenness.

5.1.1.2   Too little self-responsibility results in directionlessness and impressionability, and too much in obstinacy and dogmatism.

5.1.1.3   Too much awareness results in hypersensitivity and too little in insensitivity.

5.1.1.4   Being too moral and ethical may result in preaching, not practising; too little in damage to others and unfairness.

5.1.1.5   Uncompensated balance can produce mediocrity and stasis, but too little balance, failure through overfocusing.

5.2   The Constancies have power that can be abused by the unFIT.

5.3   Habits are a result of not being guided by the Constancies.

5.4   unFIT people cannot help revealing themselves.

5.4.1   The criticisms made by the unFIT reveal their own weaknesses.

5.5   FIT people are noticeable by their camouflage and power.

6.0   Personal goals are more difficult to decide than to achieve.

6.1   (Inner) FITness™ provides its own inner and outer direction.

6.1.1   The unFIT look for direction instead of FITness.

7.0   FIT people have a future, not a past.

7.0.1   The future is not the past continued.

7.0.2   Now is a better predictor of the future than is the past.

7.0.3   FIT people have learned from their pasts to change their futures.

7.1   A FIT person controls themselves and therefore their future.
7.1.1   This gives them control in the world.

7.2   unFIT people have a past, and possibly no future.
7.2.1   The past does not determine the future (of the FIT).

7.3   The past will return unless there is personal intervention.
7.3.1   unFIT people imprison themselves by their pasts.
7.3.2   unFIT people do not notice that the past has returned.
7.3.3   FIT people can intervene, the unFIT only think they can intervene.

7.4   A FIT person knows why what happened happened and why what is going to might.
7.4.1   There is nothing that surprises the FIT person.
7.4.1.1   Many things surprise the unFIT.
7.4.2   FIT people interrogate the now with the past past and the future now; the unFIT interrogate the now with the past and don't get as far as the future.
7.4.3   The FIT know why, the unFIT don't question.

7.5   A person has more control over an event distant in time than one soon.
7.5.1   This is because of the chains of the past.
7.5.1.1   History chains are stronger the longer they are, but future chains weaker the longer they are.
7.5.2.   A FIT person has no history chains.

8.0   FIT people do not have personalities. They behave appropriately.
8.0.1   Personality is a description of past chains and constraints.
8.0.2   Personalities could be labelled according to the habits people have.
8.0.3   People may naturally have personality.
8.0.3.1   They would benefit from FITness.

8.1   FIT people do not have habits.

9.0   FIT people can fit into any situation.
9.0.1   FIT people behave appropriately.
9.0.2   They do so comfortably.

9.1   Behaving appropriately means behaving according to the needs of the situation rather than the needs of personality.

10.0   FITness is knowing yourself and always behaving accordingly.

10.0.1   Behaving accordingly is the same as behaving appropriately.

10.1   People who are uncomfortable in situations will pay twice: then and later.

10.1.1   unFIT people have a narrow behavioural *Comfort Zone* and a large *Discomfort Zone*.

10.1.1.1 The unFIT are always being double charged and in double jeopardy.

10.1.1.2 The unFIT cannot feel the difference between unacceptable behaviour and appropriate behaviour.

10.1.2   Getting FIT involves increasing the Comfort Zone – doing things that are good for you in all ways.

10.1.3   FIT people do not have a Discomfort Zone for appropriate behaviours.

10.1.3.1 They do for unacceptable behaviours.

11.0   Knowing yourself comes from being FIT.

11.0.1   To know a person you must know their inner properties as well as their external ones.

11.0.1.1 This applies to you too.

11.0.1.2 The inner properties of others are often more apparent than your own.

11.1   Knowing and learning from others may provide EXERcise, but it cannot make someone FIT, nor give them self-knowledge.

11.2   The real self is the FIT self.

12.0   FITness builds bridges to positive universes, unFITness to negative ones.

12.1   A small thought can change an entire world.

13.0   It costs nothing to be FIT but the commitment to shape the world yourself.

CHAPTER TWO

What is (Inner) FITness™?

Are you a prisoner of your history?

Would you rather be a prisoner or a free person?

Most people would say they would prefer to be free. Those who prefer imprisonment are incarcerated by a sick or socially disabling condition. Yet it is a central contention of *(Inner) FITness*™ that most people are imprisoned. And what is worse, they are themselves the tough gaoler. Instead of learning in a beneficial way from their history and experiences, the great majority of individuals become more and more bound by their learning and cannot use it to their benefit. The good (learning) becomes bad. The potential benefits get turned into personal liabilities. The keys to change and success are used to lock the individual in an ever-tighter grip and an increasingly impregnable gaol. The free get transformed into the imprisoned.

There are many reasons for this transformation – many reasons why people imprison themselves. Circumstances are difficult for some. They are born into poor environments, they do not have the benefit of good teaching, they work in a difficult organization, they suffer a bad experience – perhaps even at the hands of their parents – and do not recover their potential, they are not very bright and do not have good skills, or they get into bad company. To many, circumstances appear to conspire against them. They get kicked when they are down whereas those who are better off seem to get the rub of the green. Instead of getting easier, life becomes harder and harder, more unpredictable, and more negative. They attract bad luck, or so it seems. The spiral never seems to turn positive. The ambiguous always turns out bad. People learn the comforts of self-imprisonment.

What about you? Are you emotionally dependent or emotionally free? Do you even know the difference? Do you behave in ways you wish you did not or are you happy with what you have done for yourself? Do you wish you had done something else with your life so far or have your achievements made you feel better inside? Do you feel that your life options are somewhat limited or are they limitless? Are you fixed in your ways, or are you flexible and open to ideas? Is your life governed by your job or are your work and social life in balance? Do things in life conspire against you or are you in charge? Do you believe in luck and fate or that you make it? Do you feel you are getting older or that age is in the head? Do the demands of your work outstrip your capacity to cope, or do you take it in your stride?

If your answer to any of these is the first of the two options you, too, are a prisoner of your history. But it gets worse. You are also in danger of becoming more constrained by your future, instead of freed by it. You will not only be limited by your past learning, but you will also be locking off doors you might have been able to enter in the future. You are becoming bound by your past and imprisoning your future. These bonds are strong, often invisible, and ever more constraining. It is an interesting thought that people have more control over what will happen to them in one year's time than in the next minute, yet they expend more effort trying to manipulate what they cannot rather than what they can control.

Figure 2.1 shows some of the external forces that are constantly acting to constrain people to be a certain way. We call these forces the 'Killing Fields' because they are always pulling at the individual to try to disintegrate their own identity or personal integrity. These forces are not necessarily bad influences – we should all learn as much from our experiences as possible, for example – but they are factors which play a role in putting us under pressure to act in certain ways, even if these are not the ways we would naturally wish to, or ways which are not good for us.

Everyone succumbs to these external pressures. But most do not realize the extent to which they do it to themselves – the degree to which they are responsible for chaining themselves to these 'external railings'. On the contrary. A well-established psychological process is that human beings tend to attribute bad things to factors outside themselves and good things to themselves. So we even explain these problems away by looking for reasons outside ourselves. Our psychological processes are very good at self-defence and self-deceit: it does not apparently pay the species to have real self-knowledge. At least not if we are happy to become biological victims in the same way that lower animals are. But we are human beings who are missing one important link in our individual progress and development: the control the individual can have over their own destiny.

FIGURE 2.1 The Killing Fields: the unFITness forces

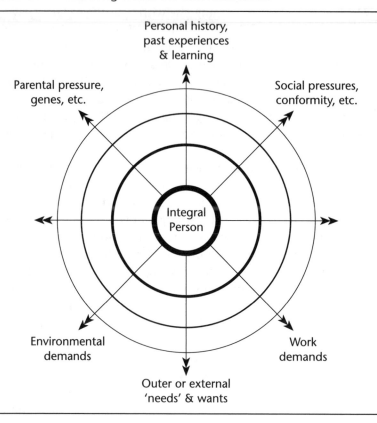

(Inner) FITness™ is about regaining that personal control. It is about bucking the inherent conservatism of the species in favour of maximizing the potentials of the individual. It pays the individual to fight against the psychologically imposed constraints whose natural tendency is to imprison and limit. (Inner) FITness™ is about how to marshal future experiences for your own benefit, instead of allowing them to close the options even further. It is about putting the individual in control. It is about abandoning notions of luck and limits, and replacing them with the potential and the positive. But it is more than that. There are many books on personal development and positive thinking. (Inner) FITness™ is different because it is not based on myths and exhortation, but on a developed theory. (Inner) FITness™ presents a structured and integrated overview of the ways in which the various components of the theory are linked and how these relate to established knowledge. In many ways, the ideas espoused here offer a reorientation and reinterpretation of psychological theory. In that sense it is a 'grand theory' of the psychology of people.

FIT for nothing?

The central notions of *(Inner) FITness*™ are contained in what we call 'FIT theory', or the 'FIT framework'. FIT is an acronym for 'Framework for Internal Transformation' or 'Flexible, Innovative and Trainable'. This section is entitled 'FIT for nothing?' to draw attention to the fact that it costs nothing to get FIT, other than a personal investment to become FIT and have the trappings of that success, financial as well as personal.

FITness here refers to psychological or mental fitness, including such aspects as emotional autonomy, awareness, incisiveness, and the ability to deal with situations and people in an appropriate manner. We distinguish between people who are FIT and those who are unFIT. A FIT person will be:

- Adaptable

- Flexible

- Receptive

- Innovative

- Unstressed and psychologically fit

- Self-developmental

- Able to respond appropriately

- Able to fit into different social and work contexts

Essentially a FIT person can *FIT* themselves to the demands of the situation. They will be healthier, more satisfied, more able to cope with all situations, and more productive. The unFIT will not have these abilities in good measure. Most people are unFIT and are not, therefore, making the most of themselves and their capabilities. FITness allows people to jettison their bad personal baggage, including poor or inappropriate learning as well as negative circumstances (such as poor upbringing, social class, etc.) and to develop individual talents to maximum advantage. Since it is our contention that most people are unFIT, the advantages of developing FITness are akin to being fit in a running race: no contest.

There are three different strata to FIT, as shown in Figures 2.2 and 2.3:

- Personal Integrity (which is the overall aim)
- The Five Constancies (which should guide behaviour and decisions)
- The Behavioural dimensions (which are the external or observable outcomes). These are labelled D1 to D15 in Figure 2.3.

Figure 2.3 illustrates this FITness triangle in a different way to show that the FIT person – one who has Inner Integrity – has a firm base for the way they behave, which is developed ideally through the operation and proper use of the five personal FITness guidelines called the Constancies.

A FIT person is able to vary their behaviour according to the situation needs and is not driven by habits and past ways of doing things. In the longer term they will also develop immunity from the influence of

FIGURE 2.2   The (Inner) FITness Framework Hierarchy

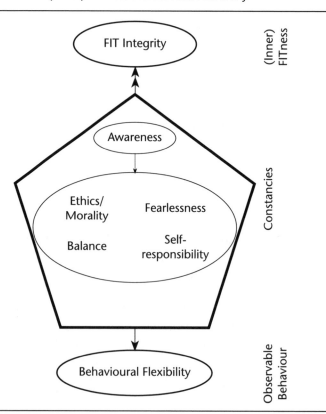

FIGURE 2.3   The (Inner) FITness triangle

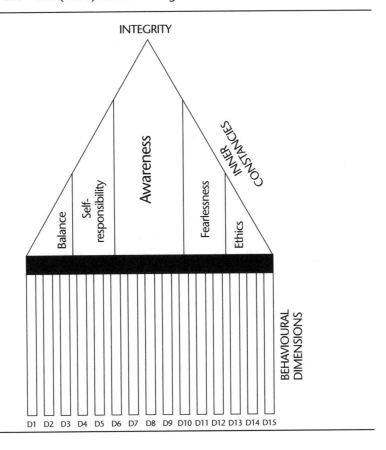

bad experiences that may have happened to them in the past. They will also be more self-contained and secure in themselves with all the attendant benefits, including being less affected by external demands and pressures.

What we call 'Integrity'

In FIT theory, a 'FIT person' is recognizable because they act at all times with what we call 'Integrity'. This provides them with a solid platform that is both respected and respectable. They have a clear set of internalized goals that are acted on in a confident manner. They behave 'appropriately' in all situations and in a way that accords with their

Integrity base. They are not swayed by temporary or short-term attractions and rewards, or put off by fear and uncertainties. Their behaviour and decisions are not dictated by random circumstances that create much superstitious, irrelevant and apparently random behaviour in others. Their Integrity provides them with personal clarity but one which is also obvious to others. The person who has Integrity will always get what they really want. The FIT person will always succeed when up against those who are less FIT.

The basis of Integrity, according to FIT theory, is that the way we live our lives minute by minute, day by day, year by year should be determined by a small number of psychological and behavioural templates that we call 'Constancies'. These are shown in Figure 2.4. These Constancy templates are the cornerstones of a large range of our behaviours and choices, including many of the unconscious processes that control much of what we do. In the unFIT, the great majority of people, these templates are incorrectly set: past experiences and other factors have shaped them in three ways that cause people to do things they should not do:

- They behave in ways that are incompatible with their real individual wants and needs. Instead, they replace these with non-individual species needs and other apparent wants which are not really relevant to them. This process is called 'Integrity misFIT'.

- They allow themselves to be seduced into behaving as they have done in the past, rather than in ways that are appropriate to the current situation or to the future needs. This process is called 'the History misFIT' or 'Learning misFIT'.

- The unFIT will base their behaviours and decisions on many other (counterproductive) factors, usually learned from their past and the Killing Fields.

FIGURE 2.4   The Constancies

- Awareness: the engine and constant monitor of FITness

- Fearlessness: the emotional manager

- Self-responsibility: the direction-giver and barometer of level of motivation

- Morality and Ethics: the social conscience manager

- Balance: the judge of emphasis given to different areas of life

---

Figures 2.5 and 2.6 represent the way the Constancies FIT together when an individual acts and decides on the basis of real Integrity, and how they lack such coherence when the person is unFIT.

Developing FITness means the psychological equivalent of getting physically fit: to make oneself more able to cope with the demands of living and working, to do this with greater ease, and to be more successful than those who are less FIT: the FIT person is in better (psychological) 'condition'. Just as the physically fit person has to engage in a healthy lifestyle to keep in trim (by not smoking, taking exercise, having a good diet, etc.), so it is necessary for the FIT person, or the one who wants to

FIGURE 2.5   (Inner) FITness: Constancies in harmony

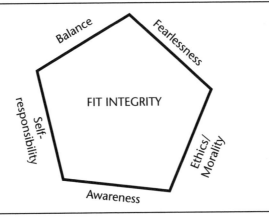

FIGURE 2.6   (Inner) unFITness: Constancies in disharmony

become FITter, to learn and use appropriately 'healthy' templates to guide their behaviour and decisions: to monitor their choices against the Constancies. This will almost certainly mean changing the basis of behaviour since their Constancy templates will have been set on the basis of past learning and previous bad decisions, as well as actions being decided according to other irrelevant and random factors. This is likely to need training, or at least education about what is necessary to do this. However, FIT thinking can soon become automatic and natural, even if temptations to backslide are always present (the psychological equivalents of chocolate cream buns and slouching around).

To be FIT an individual has to act with 'Integrity'. This means more than with moral integrity (that is why we have used the capital 'I'). It also requires taking responsibility for shaping your future, making decisions that are consistent with more appropriate Constancy templates, and actively pursuing a more positive set of behaviours. To be FIT means to try to replace decisions and behaviours which were based on external forces (these were called the 'Killing Fields' in Figure 2.1) with those which are based on the Constancies. This will allow real personal Integrity to develop. These FITness forces – the Constancies – are shown as the 'Growing Fields' of Figure 2.7. To ensure Integrity FIT there needs to be a match, or fit, between the stored (unconscious) templates and the conscious wants. Otherwise the person lacks Integrity. People who do not act with Integrity, according to FIT, will not be happy in the long term (even if they obtain outer success), they are more likely to suffer psychological problems and stress, and will be more prone to disease.

FIT theory distinguishes between wants and desires. 'Wants' are defined as those things that are truly in accord with the Constancy templates. For the FIT person these would always be moral and ethical, for example. For the unFIT, the behaviour repertoire will include the possibility of immoral actions because actions and decisions will be guided by short-term desires or random and useless criteria, rather than being 'outlawed' by appropriate and controlling Constancy templates.

The FIT person is driven by internal criteria (the pure Constancies). The unFIT are much more externally driven – they are, for example, seduced by their own egos and the outside factors that fortify these. Compare the forces of Figures 2.1 and 2.7. This also means that the unFIT will be affected more by emotional factors that have an historical root in past experiences. This process we describe as the 'emotional black hole' because it sucks people into it when they base their behaviour and decisions on past learning, rather than on an analysis of the needs of the situation. The FIT person has great stability as a result of their clear Constancy templates, but the unFIT do not. The unFIT, for example, show

FIGURE 2.7 FITness forces: the Growing Fields

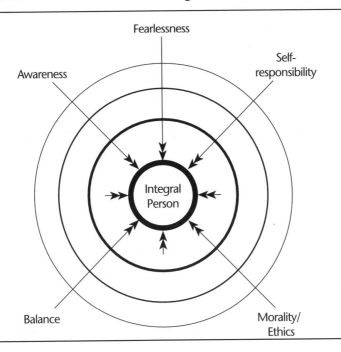

inconsistencies in actions because of the ill-formed basis of their decisions and behaviours – they may abuse their family, but would not hurt a stranger at all: they do not show consistency because of the lack of integration at the Constancy level.

It is because people do not have coherent and well-formed Constancies that they do not act in a consistent manner. Their Constancy templates are fuzzy. UnFIT people are unpredictable – 'all over the place' – in what they think and do. This does not happen to the FIT because their Constancies are well defined and clear cut, and because they are strongly internally driven. The FIT are real architects of themselves and establish their own wants and needs, independently of their history, the pressures placed on them by others and their social situation, and independently of species 'needs'. They have a true and consistent Integrity. The FIT theory puts the individual centre stage as responsible for how they are and what they do (and therefore, get).

The central motivator for the FIT individual is to act with Integrity: developing a coherent set of Constancy templates and always acting and deciding in accordance with them. There will not be compatibility between the Constancy templates for the unFIT. This will lead to inappropriate behaviours and decisions that will often be bad for the individual and those around them (e.g. their family, their work organization). These incompatibilities and inconsistencies will also reinforce themselves by the learning and repetition that naturally occur. This is one reason the FIT theory posits the need for the FIT person to be the architect. The FIT, or those aspiring to it, need to engineer the coherence. This leads to another central aspect of FITness: that of the concept of FITness as a personal growth framework in which the individual bases their decisions and behaviours on Integrity with growth.

The Constancies

There are many reasons – environmental, societal and individual – which play a role in determining the behaviours and decisions of any person. In FIT theory there are five which are considered key. These are the five Constancies, or the Constancy templates, which guide what a person does. These, shown in Figure 2.4, are:

- Awareness level: the engine and constant monitor of FITness

- Fearlessness level: the emotional manager

- Self-responsibility level: the direction-giver and barometer of level of motivation to be FIT

- Morality and Ethics: the social conscience manager

- Degree of Balance: the judge of emphasis given to different areas of life

We will consider these briefly in turn below. Chapter 7 takes a closer look at each of them.

Awareness/awakeness

This is the degree to which an individual monitors and attends to their internal and external worlds.

It is our contention that most people are not aware of what they want, why they do what they do, what they could do and become, nor their capacities and potential. They are certainly not often aware of what is happening to them minute by minute and the influences they are opening themselves up to. In consequence, the great majority of people are wasting their talents and capabilities by 'sleeping' during their waking hours: they are asleep with their eyes open. Most are driven by their automatic and learned behaviours and do not really pick up on all the feedback they could get from their surroundings and decide what would really be appropriate. Wake yourself up now and see what in your immediate environment you have missed. Consider all the sensory information from the environment around you. Interrogate how you are sitting, precisely what made you read this, how aware you have been over the past 30 seconds, the degree to which you were aware of the factors at work in the last interaction you had with someone, and so on. Unless you are very unFIT you are likely to see some of what you missed and the way in which the situation and other people determined what you sensed and did instead of you selecting what was appropriate. In a sense, we would say that people are on 'automatic pilot' most of the time. In the main, it is not their own automatic pilot, running to their own constructed programme: they do what they do without ever really thinking about it, or without ever having really thought about it. This may be generally fine, but it does not maximize potential. To be FIT a person really needs to be aware and awake. They need to take charge themselves instead of giving in to the effortless seductions of the in-built automatic pilot of the species.

This does take effort. Awareness is the engine as well as the ongoing monitor for the FIT person. Awareness is essential if a person is to develop and change proactively or non-accidentally. For the unFIT the engine is the past, and the person has their own monitor switched off most of the time. Most people are not able or willing to be attentive. In some sense one could say that they are asleep and are self-deceived in believing their inattentive state is a true one.

Fearlessness

This is acting without fear or trepidation, or essentially facing the unknown with the same bravado as the known.

The second Constancy is Fearlessness. This is the emotional dimension of FIT – the arena of the emotional battles that we all have. Most people spend a good proportion of their time in fear and its close cousins such as apprehension, anxiety, concern, worry and unease. The family of fear drives many behaviours and decisions that people make, although we do not usually see the extent of their effect on us. Fear has a strong grip on our unconscious actions and often does not allow our conscious thoughts into this secret. For some, fears are on the surface:

they are aware of the fact that much of what they do is guided by fear, but they cannot stop this because they do not have the necessary skills and confidence to replace fear with their own mastery. How many people do you know who do things because it is expected of them and not because it is necessary or worthwhile? How many people concern themselves with getting old, or making sure they are not too far from their known comforts? How many people do you know who are concerned about doing something out of the ordinary, or wearing different clothes, or telling the boss they are wrong, or stay late just because the others do? How many people do you know who have cocooned themselves in ways that allow little of the unknown into their lives? How many talk about doing something 'risky' (or risqué), have done so for a while, but will never actually take the steps needed? Fear has a tight grip on most of the people most of the time, although most have got used to the constraints and are even comforted by the presence of the negative feeling itself. For many, the grip is not one over their conscious processes, but they have become so tightly bound that even their unconscious decisions and behaviours are reigned in.

Fearlessness is only possible when people do what is right for the right reasons. It is important to be able to learn what a key role fear plays in your decision making and behaviours: to be able to disentangle the emotions from the decisions. This will mean feeling able to enter what we call the 'discomfort zone' – the area that is associated with doing things that are consistent with your real wants and needs but which at the present causes feelings of discomfort. This has to become part of your 'comfort zone' in the longer term if you are to live without fear. The feeling of entering this unknown should not be confused with the negative aspects of fear, which generally become the principal builder/ architect for most.

Fearlessness is psychological freedom, but not unfettered freedom. It has to be developed and maintained by conscious effort and awareness. It needs self-confidence, which can only be present with enhanced Integrity. It also needs directing by the third Constancy, Self-responsibility.

Self-responsibility

This is the degree to which an individual accepts personal accountability for their world irrespective of the impact of factors outside themselves.

The Self-responsibility Constancy is the motivator, self-limiter and mission-setter of the Constancies.

It is our contention that the majority of people have the view that the world, and the factors within it, conspire to prevent them from doing what they would like to do, or from being successful, or from having a nicer life at home and in the workplace than they do. They would be happier, more successful, fitter, eat better, not smoke, and so on, if only.... People see that things happen 'out there' which they have no control over and that these things can have marked consequences for them. They can sometimes make changes to this world in ways that affect them positively (e.g. by working hard they may get promotion) or negatively (e.g. if they commit a crime they may be punished). However, in the main, people do not see themselves as being the architects of their world: they see themselves as only being able to effect changes in peripheral ways. With this perspective people are viewed as victims of circumstance of a world mainly out of their control, of a life where 'lucky breaks' are crucial to success and being in the right place at the right time is important.

Most people see the barriers to progress not as being in themselves but in the constraints imposed on them from outside. They are ready and willing, and able, but the way things are stacked at present in their environment simply prevents them from moving in a positive direction. The ubiquitous 'they' are held responsible for many of their difficulties and failures to get on. (How many times have you heard people say 'They are responsible for...', or 'It was their fault...'). This is anathema to the FIT person who makes a working assumption that the world shapes around them and that they are responsible for everything that happens. It does not matter that this may not be true. It is a useful heuristic for making improvements.

The FIT person sees the importance of the homily 'The world (your world) is a reflection of yourself'. They see that they are responsible for their situation, and that if they can take responsibility for a greater sphere of it their influence on it will be correspondingly increased. Most people do not realize this and see themselves entrapped by the world. Most people see themselves constrained by the outside world in many ways and do not see that it is their own habits, expectations and behaviours that put them on the iron tracks they are on. To some, only a derailment, or major catastrophe, would get them moving in another direction – yet the number of paths a person could go down is probably infinite. We like the comfort zone of dependence. We like not exercising the freedom and control we have. We like chaining ourselves to an outside world. We like not being responsible. It does not have to be like this.

For the FIT person, luck does not happen accidentally – they construct it. The world is their chewing gum. It is their own teeth that shape it. The FIT believe in the idea that if you think as a victim you will become one. Think as a leader and you will learn to lead. For the FIT person their world is also their choice and this means that they must take great care and attention to ensure that they make decisions and behave in accordance with the way they wish it to be. This also involves the other Constancies, especially awareness and attention, since what a person properly attends to they can be said to be responsible for in some sense. This is central to key ideas in personal and business contexts such as 'owning problems' and 'empowerment'. But in an important sense it is also true that a person can only possess what they take responsibility for. Only when something is within the span of attention and awareness can it begin to take shape and become a reality. If it is not within the span of attention it cannot grow.

The influence of this Self-responsibility Constancy is deep rooted since research shows that all individuals create their own ways of looking at the world (sometimes called 'schema' or 'schemata' or 'storygrammars'). These schemas influence what people see and how they see (we have to be selective and to guide how our sensory and cognitive apparatus works, given the complexity and vastness of information we are presented with at every moment). They also determine how our memories store the experiences we have. The schemas determine the shape of history as well as future perceptions. It is now clear that human beings cannot be considered neutral experiencing and storage machines: their schema, history and personal biases are key to the 'what, how and why' of what happens to them. It is important for us to control how we use our senses and how our experiences are stored away in the unconscious recesses. If we do not take such responsibility it is likely that our past learning will exert too much influence on the future at the cost of our individual control. The more such matters can enter the sphere of personal control, the more likely it is that people can construct their futures.

Morality and Ethics

This is differentiating right from wrong and doing what is right.

The Morality and Ethics Constancy provides the social dimension, or external conscience, to set the limits for behaviour and decisions that individuals make.

A FIT person is a moral and ethical person who endeavours to make every decision an ethically and morally correct one. They do not allow external pressures to compromise moral and ethical standards. The FIT person would not do anything they considered wrong or unethical in order to achieve an external goal. Success is never at the expense of others, or of morals, in this sense.

Precisely what moral and ethical guidelines form the Constancy template will be partly individual, but they are likely to include such things as:

- treating the thoughts, desires and actions of all people with due respect;

- respecting the physical, intellectual and emotional space of all;

- having an honourable and respectful view of oneself and others;

- appreciating the rights of others;

- not being prejudiced or using stereotypes to judge others.

Balance

Making sure each aspect of life receives due care and attention. The important parts should have a sufficient level of effort put into them and the person receive sufficient satisfaction from them.

The Balance Constancy provides the voice of judgement and reasoning to explicit decisions about how people manage the varied and diverse relationships in their lives. Balance is the integration and symmetry of the various important dimensions of a person's life: ensuring that the proper focus – due care and attention – is given to each. Many people live lives that are out of balance because they are too embroiled in one area to the detriment of others.

FIT people balance the demands of the important dimensions of their lives. For most people this will include:

- work (labour);

- non-work or domestic, social and personal (people);

- the self dimension (self).

A person should endeavour to achieve a harmony, balance and symmetry between these central dimensions to ensure inner balance, as well as balance between the external elements (e.g. home and work). Balance is ensuring that no one area is dominant.

A person is unFIT if, for example, they are primarily one-dimensional, or do not have balance between the various dimensions relevant to them. For example, an imbalance will occur if a person is too self-absorbed, or if they devote too much time to a hobby, or if they are workaholic, or too focused on their children or family. FIT people are multi-dimensional in the sense that they see the importance of all dimensions and strive to achieve balance within each dimension and between the different dimensions. Within each dimension there will be a need to achieve balance between the various aspects involved. In the non-work sphere, for example, this might require achieving a balance between:

- partner;

- children;

- friends;

- leisure activities;

- wider community aspects.

The brief descriptions of each of the Constancies is recapped in Figure 2.8.

FIGURE 2.8 The Constancies described

- Awareness/awakeness:
  This is the degree to which an individual monitors and attends to their internal and external worlds.

- Fearlessness:
  This is acting without fear or trepidation, or essentially facing the unknown with the same bravado as the known.

- Self-responsibility:
  This is the degree to which an individual accepts personal accountability for their world irrespective of the impact of factors outside themselves.

- Morality and ethics:
  This is differentiating right from wrong and doing what is right.

- Balance:
  Making sure each aspect of life receives due care and attention. The important parts should have a sufficient level of effort put into them and the person receive sufficient satisfaction from them.

(Each operates both consciously and unconsciously).

Behavioural Flexibility and enhanced behavioural repertoire

When in different environments, or interacting with different people, individuals behave in ways that are particular to that situation, whether appropriate or not. Often the way people behave is based more on personal history than appropriateness. The range of these behaviours is likely to be very different between environments. In general, however, learning theories have shown that people take the path of least resistance. They do what their learning histories dictate. These learning histories determine the structure of the behaviour of individuals and determine what the path of least resistance is. FIT theory provides a structure to break the grip of these learning histories. Tackling problems without this kind of framework is bound to fail. Certainly, positive thinking itself will not do the job.

Our behaviours are very important, not only because of the effects they have on others (verbal and non-verbal behaviours), but because they provide our 'fingerprint' and our personal structures. These behaviours soon become 'automatic' in the sense that we do not cognitively heed or attend to what we say, do and behave. These 'behaviour habits' are the bain of FITness because they have outcomes for us without our noticing. Many of these outcomes will be negative because we have not properly engineered what we want and how we want to be. The negative effects will happen to us and to others with whom we interact.

Our behaviour habits:

- were learned in the past;

- are often inappropriate for us and others with whom we interact;

- are often not relevant to our present situation (e.g. work);

- are child-given, or other-given, templates for adult needs;

- impact negatively on how we feel;

- impact negatively on others and how we are perceived.

New behaviours may feel uncomfortable because old behaviours become habitual and mask what people should do. For example, people may work too many hours, which damages their health, makes them less effective and affects their personal life, pulling it out of balance. Or, perhaps someone learned to be assertive in one context and continues in that vein in a different situation when it is entirely inappropriate.

At the base of the FITness triangle (Figure 2.3) is the way we actually behave. This is the primary determinant of how others see us and the main way in which we influence others. The Constancies are responsible for this and so it is important that people take responsibility for their behaviours by altering, over time, their Constancy template profiles. The aim of FITness is always to behave appropriately and to take account of the situational demands instead of natural learned behavioural inclinations that may be inappropriate. For most people, developing FITness will mean increasing their behavioural repertoire so that they are able to do this. Learning of this kind requires awareness that behaviours also affect how people feel and perceive themselves, so that changing behaviours can have a real impact on feelings and thoughts. Two aspects are important here:

- There is often a 'feelings lag' between behaviour and the feelings they evoke in the individual: new behaviours will feel strange and even inappropriate and this 'feelings lag' will need to be considered by those who are in training for FITness.

- When a person is learning to become FIT their new behaviours may be considered inappropriate by others (just because they are new to colleagues). This needs to be predicted and accommodated.

Some people feel more comfortable in one environment than they do in another and are likely to behave accordingly. This feeling of comfort or discomfort is an important factor that influences personal behaviour in different contexts. For most people their 'comfort zone' will be different in different environments, or when with different people. It is likely to influence not only how people behave, but also how effective the interactions are for both individuals, as well as any consequential decisions and actions.

For FITness it is important to increase behavioural flexibility to act appropriately in the situation, rather than according to feelings of comfort or discomfort. FITness proposes a whole array of reasons why this is likely to be beneficial to the person, or their company, family, or whatever. Some of these will be discussed in Chapter 3.

Behavioural dimensions

In *The FIT Profiler*™, which is a diagnostic tool for assessing FITness, there are 15 different 'behavioural dimensions' which we measure. These are listed in Figure 2.9. A FIT person will show appropriate flexibility in all

FIGURE 2.9 The behavioural dimensions measured in The FIT Profiler™

• Unassertive	Assertive
• Trusting of others	Cautious of others
• Calm/Relaxed	Energetic/Driven
• Reactive	Proactive
• Definite	Flexible
• Outer-directed	Inner-directed
• Risky	Cautious
• Behave as expected	Behave as you wish
• Spontaneous	Systematic
• Single-minded	Open-minded
• Introverted	Extroverted
• Conventional	Unconventional
• Individually centred	Group centred
• Firm	Gentle
• Lively	Not lively

behavioural domains, of which these are some commonly measured examples.

In FIT theory it does not make sense to characterize people in terms of their predominant type or 'trait' characteristic, as is the norm in traditional personality theory, even though that is what the hundreds of personality tests measure. In FIT theory, a FIT person can demonstrate the behaviour at both ends of the dimensions as necessary and appropriate (i.e. they are not inflexible in their behaviour and perceptions). FIT theory measures the range of different behaviours that people can demonstrate – an indication of their behavioural flexibility, not a test of their inflexibility as measured by most tests. The 'FIT Profiler' provides you with an evaluation of your own levels of Integrity, Constancy Scores and Behavioural Flexibility.

Increasing behavioural flexibility is likely to require getting people to move outside their comfort zones. Figure 2.10 illustrates one person's comfort zone in relation to assertiveness towards those they report to. In this example the 'discomfort zone' is considerably larger than the 'comfort zone'. The position of the 'comfort zone' suggests that the person is generally at the unassertive end of the spectrum when it comes to interactions with their bosses. Figure 2.11, the same person interacting

FIGURE 2.10   The assertiveness/unassertiveness 'comfort' and 'discomfort zone' for 'people you report to'

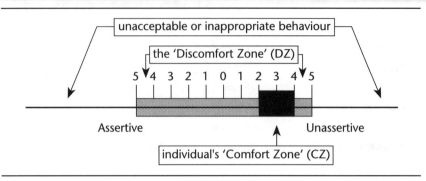

FIGURE 2.11   The assertiveness/unassertiveness 'comfort' and 'discomfort zone' for 'close friends'

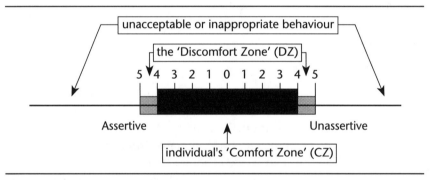

with close friends, displays a different picture. With close friends there is significantly more flexibility. The person is much more likely to display both assertive and unassertive behaviour with close friends, depending upon the particular demands of the situation.

A FIT person behaves appropriately and according to the situational demands. They determine what is appropriate with reference to the five Constancies, and not simply on the basis of their primitive feelings of discomfort or comfort. FIT predicts that by increasing behavioural flexibility in all environments, people will enjoy visible and long-lasting benefits.

One common inhibitor or barrier to increasing behavioural flexibility is the feeling associated with the 'discomfort zone'. This feeling may range from a mild negative feeling, through a mild anxiety to severe distress. The larger the 'discomfort zone', the greater likelihood of severe distress in certain circumstances.

For example, in the illustration used above, FIT predicts that the potential for real stress or strain is much greater in the 'person you report to' environment, where the spread of assertiveness is narrow, than in the 'close friends' environment where it is much larger.

Within the range of acceptable and appropriate behaviours, FIT tries to get individuals to explore their discomfort zones so that they can begin to increase the range of behaviours available for use.

With the example above, it is likely that attempting to move into either extreme assertiveness or unassertiveness in the case of 'close friends' would not present a major problem. It may not even result in a mild anxiety. However, in the 'person you report to' environment it may occasionally be necessary to be more assertive than the person generally feel comfortable with. This will be shown when they analyse each situation in terms of the Constancy criteria. However, when a person does behave in a way they are not used to, or when this is suggested, a common response is to deny the need to behave differently or simply to refuse to do it. Alternatively the behaviour change may be accompanied by a wish that one had not behaved that way. These are barriers to be overcome. In the end one wants to be in a situation of having a wider behavioural repertoire than previously and be able to act in an appropriate manner, guided only by Integrity and not old 'hard-wired' habits or feelings.

CHAPTER THREE

The personal and organizational benefits of FITness

Why wish to be FIT? Some of the advantages of being FITter will be subjective, some will be personal, some will benefit others, and yet others will be financial and economic. It is not just FIT individuals who are likely to see positive outcomes of FITness. We believe that any organization which employs FIT people, or which takes a FIT approach in their selection procedures, staff development and training, will also have a competitive advantage as well as be a more congenial place to work in. There are also likely to be direct and indirect benefits on the bottom line. In the sections below we outline some of these benefits – particularly those that we have subjected to empirical research to check out our predictions, or those that we believe can be tested. Most of the advantages are not outlined – they are implicit and self-revealing over time.

Advantages for the FIT person

- *Being protected against psychological illnesses:* A FIT person would effectively be inoculated against many psychologically based illnesses, including affective disorders such as depression, and neurotic and psychotic problems that are not organically caused.

- *Having more information to work with:* Being more aware of their environment the FIT will notice more, be able to take advantage of the greater feedback they will perceive, and will, as a consequence, be more responsive to things that happen. This brings with it many obvious consequentials. If the phrase 'information is power' has a truth, the FIT will have more of both.

- *Making it happen:* FIT people take responsibility for shaping their lives and will, therefore, be more likely to have things happen to them that they want. The FIT states attract like events; unFIT states attract negative events consistent with the negative states. FITness begets positive events, but not in any magical way: they result from the positive states. FITness entails positive thinking within a 'can happen' framework, which provides the mechanisms for advantages – not just the exhortations. For the FIT, it is themselves, not 'they', who make it happen.

- *Seeing more freedom and fewer constraints:* We have found in our empirical studies that FITter people perceive that they have more autonomy or discretion in their workplace than less FIT workers. They also see fewer constraints in their environment. Since, therefore, the FIT are more positive about what others see as negatives, they will also be less affected negatively by such apparently negative work and environmental factors. They will not suffer as much from environmentally produced or caused stress. This should not be taken to indicate that the FIT are not affected by such environmental factors. On the contrary, since the FIT are more sensitive to their environment, any beneficial changes in it should produce even greater benefits from the FIT due to their greater awareness levels and responsivity.

- *Performing better:* They will perform tasks with a greater degree of success and will, therefore, do better. Our research has shown that performance can be enhanced by a good 10 percent and in many situations significantly more. The advantages are likely to be greater in the situations that require greater personal flexibility. Since life success requires personal flexibility and application, FIT people will achieve greater life successes. They will do this with an inner integrity (that is the basis of *(Inner) FITness*™) and not at great personal cost. We would not only predict that FIT people will be more successful and happier than the unFIT, but also that successful unFIT people will not, generally, be satisfied. There are many successful but unfulfilled people. We would suggest that the only way they can become more fulfilled is to shift the basis of their actions more in line with FITness: they need to have integrity shifts, as described in Chapter 8 (section on *The Real Self and Personal Integrity*). These integrity shifts would be more appropriately described as *Integrity-shifts* in FITspeak.

- *Sharing the benefits of self-actualizers:* The FIT will share many of the benefits that Abraham Maslow attributed to self-actualizers – those at the pinnacle of the motivation hierarchy (see Chapter 9, section on *Personal Potential*). Essentially they have the ability to be more independent, tolerant of change and difference, involved with what they do, and to gain from their environment and those in it. FITness and self-actualization, however, are not the same.

- *More efficient strategy-management:* FIT people do not do better because they are just better time managers who can properly prioritize the tasks they need to do. The FIT person does better because they are likely to use more effective *strategies* in their everyday living and work. Our research has shown that FIT people, for example, learn differently. Instead of using less effective 'surface level' strategies, which the unFIT tend to adopt, the FIT individuals use multiple and deeper strategies. This means that they are more likely to find and use the appropriate way to tackle a problem or issue.

- *Getting noticed:* FITness in an individual is noticeable to others. We have found that FITter people are preferred in interview situations so that they are more likely to be successful in job interviews. For example, in one major international company in which we gave the *FIT Profiler*™ to all applicants for a graduate recruitment round, the 20 or so chosen by the different interviewers had 50 percent higher overall FITness scores, compared to the 50 unsuccessful candidates. The *FIT Profiler*™ score was much more discriminable than other psychometric tests used. We have now observed this kind of result in other selection situations too – the FITter the person, the more they are favoured by the selectors.

- *Suffering less stress and living longer:* In studies we have found that FITter individuals are happier, more satisfied, and show lower levels of anxiety and depression. We expect that (Inner) FITness will be associated with better physical health and longevity too.

- *Having more appropriate and flexible behaviours:* One reason for believing that FITness is associated with well-being is the way the FIT are likely to perceive and respond to stressful situations and demanding work environments. They will be generally more perceptive to the situation they are in and also more flexible in the range of behaviours they have available to cope with the issues that arise. In general, they will decide and act more appropriately. In addition, since they have greater inner integrity, they are also less likely to have to suffer dissonances and inner conflicts that arise in everyday life. For example, since the FIT act with morality and ethics they will not have problems arising from having to 'live on the moral edge'.

- *Benefiting from positive inner flow experiences:* The FIT person will naturally experience the positive benefits of what have been called 'flow' experiences in their everyday lives because they are more actively involved in it. They will not, however, suffer the negatives of flow that we discuss in Chapter 9: they will not be insensitive to their environment during these flow feelings because they do not lose themselves to the flow: they remain alert to necessary information and feedback that occurs.

- *Greater emotional intelligence:* The FIT should not be less emotional than the unFIT (on the contrary, they will really experience emotion), but they are more able to make a detached evaluation of situations and to use their emotions in a positive and more evaluative manner. They experience the emotions but do not get sucked into the emotional black holes in the way the unFIT are prone to. The FIT are more emotionally intelligent.

- *Cognitive flexibility:* Behavioural flexibility is an external manifestation of FITness. Greater FIT Integrity also brings with it enhanced creativity, tolerance of ambiguity, less contextually constrained thinking, and the ability to show more 'field-independence' in judgements and decisions (this is the ability to be less swayed by contextual information which might lead to particular choices). These cognitive benefits arise for two reasons. First, we have found in several studies that stress is associated with greater cognitive inflexibility: those working people with higher levels of anxiety, for example, show greater restrictions in their ability to make accurate semantic categorizations of simple words. These types of cognitive effects show that there will be indirect benefits of greater FITness. Second, we would also predict a number of direct cognitive benefits because FIT people have higher levels of awareness and receptivity to relevant information.

- *Stopping personal history repeat itself:* The FIT do not recycle their past, as is common for the many: in FITness, present considerations decide. Thus a major advantage of being FIT is not getting caught up in the negative cycle which enmeshes many – the repetitions of personal history. It is our contention that many personal problems and dysfunctions are due to a failure of people to perceive these repetitions and their personal consequences before it is too late.

For many people, at a personal and social level, life becomes a cycle of repetition and habit, not renewal and change. We see the FIT person as one who *evolves*, while the unFIT tends to *revolve* and to revisit the same situations in the same inappropriate ways. Addictions are an extreme form of history failure. FIT people will not be prone to physical or psychological addictions such as alcohol and work. There are, however, many ways in which the unFIT recycle history. For example, they do as those before them did (and say that that is good in its own right), they are dominated by habits and past behaviours, they pass their histories on to their children, and they shape their futures with their contaminated pasts. The FIT use only the good aspects of the past and provide their children with skills and opportunities.

- *The FIT learn from criticisms they and others make:* The FITter an individual is, the more information they can utilize effectively. The FIT are more receptive to feedback from the world around them, from others and from their own thoughts and behaviours. One aspect of behaviour that can provide valuable insights into some-one's way of thinking is what they say. We do not mean the obvious about what they say, but rather what is behind what is said. For example, a powerful tool is to make the assumption that when a person is being critical of someone else, or of something they have done, the structure of the criticism reflects the weaknesses of the speaker. People unwittingly reveal their own weaknesses, problems and personal issues when they discuss things external to themselves. They give themselves away when wishing to reveal the weaknesses of another. This can equally be applied to the FIT person too: what they say also reveals their weaknesses. They will make use of this self-revealed information to improve themselves, as well as to learn about the Achilles' heels of others. It is a salutary lesson indeed to listen and analyse what you say in this way.

Advantages in the social domain

The FIT invest in themselves, but others also receive the dividends. This occurs in a number of ways:

- *Family growth and caring:* The FIT will be more attentive in their family lives than the unFIT and will develop themselves and their family alike. They will not have an unhealthy focus on work to the exclusion of home, and their balanced priorities also ensure that they give sufficient time to themselves to provide self-development and growth for their own and others' benefit. It has been found in research that there is a tendency for like to marry like. It appears, for example, that shorter men marry shorter women, and that those who marry tend to be from similar jobs, social classes and religions and to have similar leisure and other interests. More surprising, perhaps, is that those who marry also have similar blood pressure levels and biological risk profiles. It would be expected that FITter men would attract FITter women and vice versa. The children of the FIT may also turn out FITter for reasons of nature and nurture. FITness is probably an attractive characteristic with the many and varied consequences this has.

- *Enhanced social intelligence:* FIT people are more socially intelligent than the unFIT: they are more able to use social cues to assist them in their endeavours and to see the needs of others. This does not mean that they are necessarily more conciliatory, or 'softer', than others. What they do they do because it is judged appropriate, not because it is 'easy'. In this sense, they are also more socially independent: social pressures affect them less than they do others. They should be less prejudiced (since that is a history-bond) and more accepting of social differences.

- *Positive social stress carriers:* Our research has shown very clearly that stress can be passed to others who are not directly exposed to the negative environments. People can act as stress carriers, even if they are not affected by the stress themselves. For example, occupational stress can be transmitted from men to their wives so that they share their occupational mortality risks. Thus, it is possible to predict a married woman's life expectancy, and her cause of death, by knowing what her husband's direct occupational risks are. We have shown this across some 550 different occupational groupings and over 20 or so diseases (for more detail, the reader could see Professor Fletcher's book, *Work, Stress, Disease & Life Expectancy*). We have also shown that the day-to-day stresses in the workplace can be transmitted between marital partners (this research was published in volume 69 of the *Journal of Occupational & Organizational Psychology*). The FIT will infect others with the benefits of FITness and not transmit the negative consequences of unFITness to them.

- *Social Integrity:* The FIT do not try to take advantage of others, or to hoodwink them. They act morally and ethically and do not like sharp practices. They do not take the view in social interaction that there needs to be winners and losers. If possible, both can win without either party taking a position of compromise.

- *Winners:* The FIT win. They are seen as winners. Others want to emulate them. And they do all this with Integrity.

Advantages for the organization

Organizations that have an identifiable personality, culture or climate are not FIT because the culture will, at least sometimes or to some degree, determine the response of the organization to business, market, or other external demands. This response may be appropriate – it may even be that the organization has managed to build a culture that suits its market and position to a large extent. It is inherently difficult, however, to continue to ensure that the culture is one that remains fit to the task as conditions change. This has led Human Resource experts and management gurus to offer many management-led initiatives that keep the company up to the game. It used to be Time Management, Job Redesign, Management-By-Objectives, Autonomous Working Groups, Customer-Focused Management, Total Quality Management, Concurrent Engineering and Re-engineering. There are many hundreds of such initiatives peddled by one or another expert, and taken up by organizations to different degrees. It may be that we are now moving towards Knowledge Management with the expansion of the IT age. These fads have come and gone (or will go) and perhaps from time to time get relabelled and recycled. I would call them 'organizational-initiative leviathans' because they are hungry monsters that need continual feeding with resources. They produce, at best, only marginal improvements. Their value is inherently limited if only because the context of business and management is constantly changing and being redefined. The shelf life of each such management-led initiative gets less and less.

These initiatives, or movements, are ineffective to the degree to which they do not encompass the elements of the FIT perspective. They are also successful to the degree to which they do. The key element in FIT is the focus on the individual as opposed to the organization. However, *(Inner) FITness* can offer a prescription for organizational development at the same time as rejecting initiatives that are managerially homogeneous.

A FIT organization is defined by the FITness levels of the employees and not by the degree to which it can proceduralize, systematize and document management initiatives. To develop and become FITter, an organization needs just to develop gradually the *(Inner) FITness* of some or all of its employees. We suggest that the degree to which it fails to do this, and the areas in the organization where FITness levels are lowest, will reflect in the problems and needs of the organization. Unlike most initiatives, however, any improvement in any part of the organization will begin to reap benefits: there are no hidden costs, or problems with areas that are or are not tackled.

At the organizational level there are many aspects of FIT that will produce benefits. It is our view that companies should aim to make all their employees FITter, to use the FITness framework as a training and developmental tool, and to use the *FIT Profiler*™ as a selection device to supplement or replace other psychometric instruments used. A company that takes the (Inner) FITness approach would be one whose individuals were more likely to be FIT. We would call a FIT company or organization a FIT Corporation™. The FIT Corporation™ has many potential advantages. Some of these are shown in Figure 3.1.

In Figure 3.1, the *FIT Corporation*™ – one that employs FITter people – is contrasted with what we call the *polar culture* which is typical of most organizations. The polar culture is the way in which many organizations can be categorized according to one or other of the culture and climate descriptions which represent the values and implicit structures defining the social and psychological character of the company: in some sense the personality traits of the organization. The *FIT Corporation*™ leaves no such organizational imprints because it has a culture that changes with the needs of the business: a FIT culture. This will be:

- *A self-developmental organization:* The *FIT Corporation*™ is naturally receptive to the changes that are an integral aspect of modern business. It will be a self-learning organization in a true sense – not one that needs the imposition of another management-led fad to take it forward. The development of the polar organization needs to be taken slowly and changes made incrementally if they are to be successful within their context.

- *Transforming, not static:* A FIT person, like any other, needs the right context and work environment to do well for themselves and the organization. They do not, however, have to be managed constantly to do the job. They have a 'can do' perspective, and not a 'cannot because...' mentality. They can self-manage if their goals are clear and accepted. They are also likely to be transformational leaders and

FIGURE 3.1   The FIT Corporation™ culture

	A FIT culture	A polar culture
Receptivity to change	Adaptable; flexible; change without pain	Rigid; powerful status quo; shift requires pain
Management	Transformational; self-organizing; autonomous; empowering	Transactional; constant steerage; intervention critical
Organizational disorders	Apparent inconsistency; superior 'look'; self-blame	Self-destructive; depressed; abnormal response; delusion and self-deceit; fault projection outwards
Ethics	Constant; self-responsible; ethical	Ethical management focus needed to limit business drivers
Action culture	Can do	Could do (if)
Innovation and initiatives	Natural	Only if chaos (Stacey); needs managing (but cannot?)
Information flows	Fast; organic; natural understanding of difference	Retentive; 'information is power'
Learning organization	Insightful; creative; step-changes and shifts	Incremental learning possible
Dissonance and misfit	Minimal	Always present
Problem solving	Awareness and responsibility for issues; solution-focus	Depends on skills and training; problem-focus
Quality control	From individual outwards; natural	Managed control processes only; forced
Stability	Bounded instability but stable when challenged	Apparently stable until challenged, then unstable
Leadership potential	Natural, inherent	Forced (square pegs)
Politics of organization	Irrelevant or supportive	Diplomacy and political games; destructive shadow politics
Power	At all levels	Hierarchical; in managers
Performance	Inherent; constant	Requires carrots; tires
Development	Growth-led	Management-led

managers themselves, instead of relying on the old carrot-and-stick management techniques employed by the transactional managers.

- *Inherently strong:* The *FIT Corporation*™ is stable, although it may appear to have what we call 'bounded instability'. By this we mean that its responsiveness and flexibility may give the appearance of instability because of the fact that there may not be as much homogeneity of culture across the organization and a greater degree of local employee discretion and managerial style. This is not an actual instability, however, in any sense – it has a very stable core that is resistant to exterior business challenge because of its integrity and flexibility. The local variations should exist to better match the business needs and individual styles that exist. On the other hand, the polar culture may appear to be stable but is not. In the polar culture, power is in pockets (e.g. managers, shareholders or wherever) and the organization built or developed for its market or business niche. If that niche is compromised in any way (fashions change, or new competition from at home or abroad) the organization finds it difficult to readjust. When challenged, the old power base becomes unstable and sometimes initiatives take too long to put in place to readjust to business demands. Moreover, in the *FIT Corporation*™ the spread of power ensures minimal dissonance between individuals (because FIT people are self-responsible, even if following instructions and directives). In the polar culture, however, dissonance is always present because it is a natural consequence of polar cultures where individuals do not feel truly empowered and self-responsible.

- *Information rich:* The *FIT Corporation*™ is 'information rich' in the sense that messages spread quickly. FIT people are receptive and alert to relevant information and act on it rapidly. Innovation and creativity are a natural consequence of the enhanced flexibility of the *FIT Corporation*™. In the polar cultures, however, a great deal of useful information and knowledge is simply not noticed and managed – and even well-documented aids and procedures not read. Moreover, innovation and positive change can only occur as a consequence of what our colleague, Professor Ralph Stacey, calls 'chaos management'. In his book *Managing Chaos*, he shows that the sub-cultures that exist in what we label polar-type organizations are responsible for the real innovation that occurs. The sub-cultures are the informal information flows and alliances that fill the vacuums left by the formal power and organizational structures. In a *FIT Corporation*™ these sub-cultures would not exist.

CHAPTER FOUR

Recognizing unFITness

Not many people are FIT. This implies they are not making the most of themselves, nor being as useful to themselves, their family or their organization as they could be. It also implies that they will find life more stressful and difficult, they will be less creative and more intolerant of uncertainties which should provide the spice to living. Some people would say with confidence that they are FIT and that they are getting much from a successful life. It is probably true that those people who say they are would be quite unFIT and know this inside, or cannot admit it even to themselves because of the fragility of their inner selves: they cannot afford to rock that boat because it would let waves in. The FIT always know there is more self-work to be done, and do not find they have a need for self-aggrandizement in the company of others: their FITness is a private inner matter, not something to be displayed in public.

This chapter is about the different ways in which people are unFIT. It presents a number of categories of unFITness – based on the FIT framework of the previous chapter – with a view to helping people recognize the areas they may need to work on. With physical fitness, there may be different ways in which a person can work to improve their fitness, including building muscle strength, improving suppleness, developing stamina, or being more motivated. To obtain targeted benefits individuals need to concentrate in certain areas – be it tailored training regimes, altering diet, quitting smoking, losing weight, strength or stamina training or whatever. Chapter 6 offers some guidelines to improve *(Inner) FITness*™ levels, depending upon the diagnostic outcomes from doing your own *FIT Profiler*™ (see next chapter) and how you see yourself in relation to the categories outlined in this chapter.

Lack of FITness will usually present itself as a failure to act with sensitivity in a situation. That is, a failure to exhibit a required behaviour in order to obtain the maximal mutual benefits from it. In the main, this will exhibit itself in terms of a constriction or restriction in behavioural repertoire, so that the inappropriateness of the behaviour is apparent in any unbiased appraisal of it. The limitations are usually revealed as personal limitations rather than situational ones – someone else could have made more out of the situation, or the person themselves could have done so with more thought (i.e. a more Constancy-driven, rather than personal-history-driven approach). More unusually a person may exhibit too much flexibility and this is equally problematic when the behaviour is not guided by appropriate personal constraints.

Types of unFITness

Figure 4.1 presents some of the more common categories of unFITness.

Integrity unFITness

In terms of misFIT at the level of Integrity, there are several types:

- *History or Learning MisFIT*: The past wins out over the need. This is when a person bases their behaviour and decisions on springs of

FIGURE 4.1 Types of unFITness

Integrity unFITness:

- History or Learning MisFIT: the past wins out over the need
- Integrity misFIT: not being guided by real wants and needs
- Novice MisFIT: not yet mastered FITness, but trying

Constancy unFITness:

- Insufficiently developed Constancies – low measures of Fearlessness, Balance, Self-responsibility, Morality and Ethics, and Awareness
- Lack of balance between the five Constancy levels
- A dislocation between the Constancies and behaviour
  - due to a lack of motivation
  - overfocusing on either internal or external information – insularity or externality

Behavioural unFITness:

- Inflexibility
- Inappropriate flexibility

---

action from their past learning instead of an analysis of current situational need. For example, they may fall back into old habits because of current stresses. This type of unFITness plays a major role in addictions where the past habits have a biological basis as well as a psychological one. In other situations, 'this is the way it's always been done' is never a justification for doing it that way again.

- *Integrity misFIT*: Not being guided by real wants and needs. This occurs when an individual does not have clear enough ideas about what their needs and wants are, or when they allow themselves to be diverted from them in the decisions and behaviours they display. Examples would include succumbing to pressure from a boss to stay all hours, despite having worked effectively within normal times; or perhaps deciding not to do that evening class because of spouse pressure (possibly due to their fears and unFITness). This type of unFITness is very prevalent.

- *Novice MisFIT:* Not yet mastered FITness, but trying. Some people may not be naturally inclined to FITness – for many reasons – and need to test out and experiment with themselves before they can begin to get FIT. For example, they may have very limited horizons, or not be used to taking control of themselves, and will need to understand their own self-imposed boundaries and limitations. Some others may abuse their powers (the assertive level in Figure 4.3).

Constancy unFITness

The five Constancy templates are central to FITness and without high measures on them an individual cannot be FIT. The most obvious reason for unFITness is *insufficiently developed Constancies* – low scores on the scales that measure Fearlessness, Balance, Self-responsibility, Morality and Ethics, and Awareness. Low Constancies result in low Integrity, and therefore, low levels of Behavioural Flexibility. Perhaps the most damaging lack is in Awareness because this provides the engine for the operation of the others. A person needs to be aware to see the damage caused by Fear, lack of Self-responsibility, or whatever. Fearlessness will provide the courage to try (and fail occasionally), to be in the minority, to act individually, to say 'no', or to go through with the direction given by Self-responsibility.

However, having high Constancy levels does not ensure FITness for two distinct reasons:

- There needs to be a degree of *balance* between the Constancy levels otherwise behaviour may not be appropriately guided. A relatively high level on one Constancy (albeit amongst generally low Constancy levels), for example, may serve to constrain behaviours because it has overbearing consequences. For example, someone who is fearless in the extreme may do atrocious things if not sufficiently morally/ethically guided. Someone who is highly aware may focus their attention on internal aspects and become too insular, perhaps to a pathological level; or a highly self-responsible person may become workaholic if they do not pay enough attention to achieving balance between the various aspects of life.

- There may be a *dislocation* between Constancies and behaviour. Some people may have the apparatus to be FIT (perhaps akin to a good body in physical fitness) but do not make the most of it, or indeed abuse it. This dislocation might occur for three reasons:
  - There may be a lack of *motivation* to act in accordance with the Constancies. This might occur, for example, with those who have the external trappings of success, and do not want to compromise these. Some may simply be internally lazy. This could also be considered as a kind of lack of emotional intellect.
  - There may be an *over-focusing* on either internal or external information. Some people, for example, may have high levels of Integrity as measured by the Constancies, but not exhibit Behavioural Flexibility because they are not sufficiently externally focused. They may not pay sufficient attention to what they do and, therefore, not consider whether they have acted appropriately, or in line with the situation demands. To put this another way, those with high Constancy scores may not know how to use their talents to proper effect. These people do not really learn from their experiences in any progressive way: they have the experiences that only serve to imprison them further. The information gained from the experiences is not put to good effect. This is insular unFITness, or self-imprisonment.
  - They may have other *personal qualities* which mask their unFITness. For example, someone who is socially skilled or very charming may get away with cognitive and behavioural inflexibility (in the short term at least).

Behavioural unFITness

The majority of behavioural unFITness is a result of limitations in people's behavioural repertoire as a result of their natural tendency to fall back on old (restricted) habits. This happens because they are insufficiently Fearless, Aware, Balanced, Self-responsible or Moral. However, some individuals do demonstrate inappropriate flexibility that is not Constancy-led. For example, they may behave according to learned stereotypes, perhaps as a result of training or simply having observed the behaviours in others. In such cases it is unlikely that the person will be able to adapt those behaviours according to contingencies that may arise – this would really be rather shallow 'modelling' not based on any firm principles, pragmatic or otherwise.

Another way in which behaviours may appear to be flexible would be when an individual acts in a somewhat random way. They may do this when in novel situations with no referents for what to do from their past situations. Alternatively, people may act in apparently new ways when they do not know how to behave. These are both reflections of barrenness in behavioural repertoire, not richness.

Appropriate and inappropriate behaviour

A key aspect of *(Inner) FITness*™ is behaving appropriately in all situations. Inappropriate behaviour in FITness theory is when an individual does not act in accordance with the five Constancies – when they show lack of Fearlessness, Self-responsibly, Awareness of all relevant feedback from their senses and emotions, Morality/ethics, and lack of due regard to the Balance of things. Few can manage this, even fewer to any sustained extent. Most people need a 'springboard' of clear guidelines against which to compare what they decide and do. Below are set out some heuristics or practical pointers that can be kept in mind to help make the jump away from the structures of the past. The things to avoid – what we have labelled the *FITness Toxins* – are those feelings and behaviours likely to work against being FIT. Behaviours and decisions are likely to be inappropriate (as well as unFIT) if the Toxins accompany the choices made. On the other hand, the *FITness Vitamins* are likely to assist in the quest for FITness and are positive indicators that the individual is on the right track.

The Twelve FITness Toxins:

- Doing things the way you have before, without thinking
- Remembering

- Habitual behaviour and using the past as a guideline
- Being influenced by others
- Feeling as if you have no choice
- Doing things because of constraints
- Putting nothing of you into it
- Feeling stressed, or any negative feeling or emotion
- Feeling a lack of discretion and autonomy to decide
- Not really deciding, but letting it happen
- Passive acceptance
- Letting your emotions play a part in deciding what to do

The Twelve FITness Vitamins:

- Questioning
- Thinking about goals and looking forward
- Feelings of empowerment and support
- Getting, perceiving and using feedback
- Positive feelings and emotions
- Enhancing growth and development
- Feeling awake and sensitive to things
- Using your skills
- Analysing the situation
- Feeling that intuition is winning
- Being prepared for challenge and discomfort
- Using your emotions, instead of just letting them happen

The Vitamins will enrich behaviour and decisions and increase the chances that the individual will operate in line with the Constancies and develop their *(Inner) FITness*. They provide a kind of exercise regime to aid FITness. It is surprising how much self-harm people inflict on themselves by living on a diet of Toxins, yet expecting to be FIT and healthy, to be efficient and productive, to enjoy and expand themselves. Change the diet and it is likely that people will feel the benefits, even though this may take a little getting used to. Indeed, some people are so addicted to the bad things that they appear to seek the Toxins even in FIT-enriched environments. Such people need to be weaned off the dependency of the past. How many people do you know, for example, who have reached middle age (some start this very young indeed) and look back to their childhood, to their past, and begin to find great emotional value and support in it? They may buy a home where they were brought up, or go visiting the 'old haunts', and rekindle old 'friends' they have managed to find no value in for many years. Such people are trying to buy back their past. They are preparing to kill themselves by practising with the outfits of old age. This is not the way to move forward into a world of *(Inner) FITness*. It is a one-way ticket to the erosion of personal Integrity and a cocooning in the comfort of the past, instead of an opening up of new horizons and possibilities.

Inappropriate outcomes

Inappropriate decisions and behaviours are the outcomes of a person's historical schemas – the filters that are responsible for how we all perceive the world. Most people do not have well-formed Constancies to guide their outcomes because:

> *either the levels of the Constancies are generally too low (i.e. the person is very history-schema driven),*

or alternatively,

> *the outcomes are too biased by a set of Constancies that are not in harmony because one or more of them is too strong (or weak).*

If an individual's Constancy scores are generally too low, behaviours and outcomes will be generally predictable. The person will do things the way they have done so before (largely independently of the situation). They will only be appropriate if the situation is the same or similar to those commonly experienced before by the person. If any aspect is new or different – even if this may be crucial to an outcome such as making an important sale or solving a life-threatening problem – the unFIT person will adopt their past behaviours and decisions. Therefore, the more the specific situation deviates from past experiences, the more inappropriate the behaviour of the unFIT person will be. The unFIT act and decide appropriately only when the situation is one they have commonly experienced in the past. The more novel the situation, the more it is necessary for the person to be Flexible, Innovative and Trainable – to be FIT – in order to act appropriately. The higher the history/Constancy-driven ratio (i.e. the more the decisions are informed by history rather than Constancy-influenced), the less effective and appropriate will be the decisions and behaviours. So inappropriate behaviours are more likely the more unFIT the person and the more novel the situation. To become more effective – to act more appropriately – it is necessary to increase the influence of the Constancies in behaviours and decision making.

Decisions dictated by the past and not by the present produce inappropriateness. Constancy-guided decisions and behaviours can overcome this, but when the Constancies are not in harmony, this too can cause inappropriate behaviours and decisions for other reasons. Figure 4.2 illustrates the types of problems that arise for an individual when there is either too much strength, or alternatively, weakness in the various Constancy areas.

For the unFIT person it is better to work on the weaker areas first, than to develop too much strength in any particular Constancy. This serves to increase the harmony between the Constancies, and helps prevent specific weaknesses from having an overbearing effect that could become fixed.

Levels of Integrity and personal growth

Personal growth occurs when Integrity is developed, which happens when the individual's behaviour and decisions are guided by the five

FIGURE 4.2 The outcome of strengths and weaknesses in Constancies

Too much relative strength in a Constancy results in:

Constancy	Outcome
Fearlessness	Stupidity
Self-responsibility	Obstinacy/dogmatism
Awareness	Hypersensitivity
Morality	Preaching, not practising
Balance	Stasis/mediocrity

Relative weakness in a Constancy results in:

Constancy	Outcome
Fearlessness	Illness/anxiety
Self-responsibility	Directionless/impressionable
Awareness	Insensitivity/lost opportunity
Morality	Damage to others/unfairness
Balance	Failure/over-focus

Constancies and when the relationships between the Constancy templates become more consistent. For example, it is possible to behave in a fearless way but to do immoral acts, or to be very aware that the work one is doing is putting the balance between home and work out of kilter. Such behaviours are not 'FIT'. These are examples of the interactions when just two are not consistent with each other. In *(Inner) FITness* there are five levels of interaction (the Constancies) to develop consistency between.

Another way at looking at FITness is to measure what we call the 'level of integration' of the person. These different levels of integrity are shown in Figure 4.3. Effectively this means seeing enhanced Integrity as the degree of development, and integration, of the Constancies. Although 'level of integration' is a continuum, it may be useful to categorize it into different levels:

- *Level 1 – the dependent level:* Here the person is simply reactive to the situation they are in the way they have done so before, without any input from their own Constancy templates. They are externally driven and directed. At this level the person takes no responsibility, nor do they see the consequences of not doing so. They are dependent on other people and outside factors completely. These are followers or blind 'disciples'.

- *Level 2 – the victim level:* At this level the person knows that there are better states of affairs but feels they cannot change either themselves or aspects of their environment significantly. One could consider that they are like dependent Level 1s but with an added self-imposed negative spiral. They feel constrained by circumstances. They are victims.

- *Level 3 – the novice level:* Individuals at the novice level have potential. They are aware of their own powers to change things, but have not yet grasped what is needed to do that in themselves. They

---

FIGURE 4.3   The different levels of (Inner) FITness Integrity

---

- Level 1 – the dependent level: shaped by external factors

- Level 2 – the victim level: as 1, but with a self-negative spiral

- Level 3 – the novice level: experimenting with self-forces

- Level 4 – the assertive level: powerful self, but also a dangerous stage

- Level 5 – the charismatic level: powerful and (Inner) FITness

---

are self-aware and willing to experiment but are low on most of the Constancies.

- *Level 4 – the assertive level:* Here the person wants to be proactive and change things but they do not have the personal base to do so except by force, power, argument and personal charm. These people can be powerful because they have mastery and power in some areas. For this reason, people who get to the assertive level, but no further, can be successful but they are never charismatic. They lack true Integrity, but are probably strong on some of the Constancies, but these are not properly integrated or balanced. This is a dangerous level where the seductions of not developing further are greatest.

- *Level 5 – the charismatic level:* These people have both power and inner Integrity in the FIT sense. They have a personal strength that reveals itself. They are not fazed by any situation because they have a strong inner resource, based on the Constancies, which provides their firm footing. They act without fear, are always aware, act morally and ethically, have balanced lives, and take responsibility for their world.

To illustrate the level of integration ideas further a useful distinction can be made between events and states. Events are the things that happen in the 'outside' world. States are what we experience inside, including our emotions and thoughts. Those individuals at the lower levels of Integrity do not generally see that their states can cause events, but usually see the connection in reverse – the events that happen make them have certain feelings and thoughts. They do apparently make things happen by doing and behaving in particular ways and making what they believe to be choices and decisions. Those at the higher levels have a different perspective. They see that their states are responsible for the events that occur and that they experience, although there may be an invisible or lengthy delay between cause and effect. They see that there is a direct connection (what we call 'the psycausal nexus') between the state and the event. They can take responsibility for the events because they guide the states through the Constancies.

The people at the lower levels see the events that occur as being outside their control, even though they are partly mediated by their past states and their (sometimes) deliberate and (usually) unconscious prior decisions and behaviours. For the person who is at the highest level of Integrity, an accident is seen as a state waiting for the right moment to occur. For those at Level 2, the victim level, the events happened in unfortunate and unlucky isolation from their states. The person at the higher level will question why an apparent 'accident' occurs: what previous states were responsible for it, and how a different decision would have caused a different event path to happen. The Level 1 person simply experiences the events that occur, but the Level 5 person dissects their role in them – interrogates the psycausal nexus – and integrates this into future decisions. The Level 5 person owns the states and events they experience. Those at lower levels disown them to various degrees.

It is important to be aware of one's strengths and power. It is often true that those with FIT potential have power over others that they abuse, often without knowing it. Figure 4.3, for example, illustrated that those at Level 4 of Integrity/FITness – which we called the assertive level – may not be able to turn down the short-term benefits deriving from such self-power. Such individuals are powerful people and can damage others by the powers they can wield. People in positions of responsibility, for example, may be cut short in their development by these 'external' attractions and do not become FIT. They can be bullies without knowing it because they do not develop strong enough self-insight and awareness. Their effects can be marked. One workaholic boss, for example, will cause many to conform to their expectations of hours of work, despite the negative consequences on themselves, others, and the effectiveness of the organization. Unfortunately, some know they are bullies and enjoy it.

FITness layers

There are different layers to personal FITness. To be FIT an individual needs to demonstrate FITness on all the layers. The layers are displayed in Figure 4.4. Each layer interacts with every other such that FITness at any layer has beneficial effects on the other layers.

FIGURE 4.4   Layers of FITness for the individual

Biological
Physical condition
Psychological maintenance
Social independence (from others)
Independence (from the past)
Growth need
Spiritual/Intuitive

'Putting up the mirror'

In general, people reflect themselves in all that they do: in their behaviours, both verbal and non-verbal. The more unFIT people are, the more they reflect their pasts in what they do. They may not mean to but they do. This is one of the basic presuppositions of the behavioural and psychological sciences, and permeates the study of people: from the way in which their cognitive or thinking processes work when doing everyday tasks, to their most complex social behaviours and structures. FITter individuals do not reflect their pasts as much because they are more likely to act appropriately by reference to the Constancies, than simply to behave as they have done before, without due regard to situational needs.

When trying to determine how FIT a person is, one test is to see how much they criticize others, instead of accepting responsibility themselves. The unFIT will be 'other critical' – or shift blame elsewhere. The nature of their criticism is likely to reflect their own weaknesses. It is interesting to realize that criticism generally reflects the weaknesses of the critic: if you want to know the weaknesses of someone, listen to what they say are the weaknesses of others. That is true of you too. What people say and do, therefore, provides a key to their inner selves. This key is a powerful tool in itself, which the FIT can marshal for positive effect – both in self-improvement and in interpreting others.

The FIT individual is sensitive to others and to the other feedback that is available to them in their environments. Another test of FITness, therefore, is the degree to which the person takes account of this feedback in their determination of what they do. The unFIT do not perceive information and feedback and often pay too little appropriate attention to others and to their needs. The unFIT will also largely ignore their own real needs and the feedback they receive from their own inner self. Integrity is a public quality that is as noticeable when present, as when absent, in others.

FIT individuals have a more realistic assessment of themselves and situations than do unFIT individuals. This is because their schemas – the perceptual and decision filters – are not as constrained by past decisions, actions and natural tendencies. Decisions are Constancy-based, not history-based, and stand more chance, therefore, of being appropriate. Improvements in FITness will develop this objectivity in decision and action: the process of developing 'reality sensors' to replace the personal history schemas which usually dominate in the decision and action processes. Everyone has schemas – they are your world filters – but they may be inappropriately set for FITness and personal growth. The aim of the FITness programme is to break down these history schemas and replace them with reality schemas. The FITness Profiler will provide feedback about your own profile in relation to the FITness dimensions, and the areas you may need to work on. The EXERcises that follow will provide some help to improve the problem areas, although in the end it will be your own intuition and analysis allied with determination to take charge that will determine your development. Historical ties are strong and often long, but there is no necessity for them to spread their influence into the future. The ties can be broken with a small idea. That opens up options and frees you from the tyranny of the past. It leaves you in a position to design your own future rather than to be ensnared in your past.

CHAPTER FIVE

The FIT Profiler™

How FIT do you think you are?

The first part of this chapter is to find out how FIT you think you are. The second part is to get you to complete a *FIT Profiler™*, so that you can have a proper estimate. This will allow you to:

- compare your own estimates with real measures on the various FIT dimensions;

- gain some initial insights into the areas you may need to concentrate on to increase your FITness. The FIT EXERcises in Chapter 6 will help you to do that.

The purpose of the next section is for you to form a picture of how you see yourself in terms of your behavioural repertoire and the FIT Constancies. It is a highly subjective measure but you might find it interesting to do.

Please consider the way that you *behave* on a day-to-day and week-to-week basis. Do not consider how you would *like* to be or how you think others would prefer to see you. Be as objective and honest as you can. Think about how predictable your behaviour is and how someone else would judge it. Rate this on a scale of 1–100 (or a percentage) relating to the question.

1. Predictability of your behaviour

   I think that my behaviour is generally ..65.. % predictable
   (0% = behaviour totally unpredictable, 100% behaviour is totally predictable)

   Now some other questions of a general nature to be completed in the same manner:

2.   Appropriateness of your behaviour

I think that around . .*70*. . % of all my behaviours and decisions are appropriate to the situation.

3.   Overall FITness assessment

I would say my overall FIT score would be (choose one):

much lower than the average
a little lower than average
average
a little higher than average   X
much higher than the average

4.   Estimation of your levels on the Constancies

Now consider the way that you *feel* on a day-to-day basis in terms of the five Constancies. Again, it is important that you rate how you actually feel, and do not consider how you would like to feel, or how you think others would like you to be. Be as objective and honest as you can. Use a percentage scale, as in the first example above.

My level of Self-responsibility is . .*70*. . %
This is the degree to which you accept personal accountability, and take responsibility for your world and how things are for you, irrespective of the impact of any external factors or constraints.

My level of Awareness is .*60*. . . . %
This is the degree to which you monitor and attend to your internal and external worlds. How much are you really aware of everything around you and everything that happens to you?

My level of Balance is .*47*. . . %
This is making sure each aspect of your life receives due care and attention. The important parts should have a sufficient level of effort put into them and you should receive sufficient satisfaction from them if you have good balance.

My level of Morality/ethics is . .*95*. . %
This is differentiating right from wrong. How much of what you do and think is guided by moral and ethical codes?

My level of Fearlessness/self-assuredness is .*65*. . . %
This is acting without fear or trepidation, or essentially facing the unknown with the same bravado as the known. How much do you do things out of fear, rather than because you want to?

What is your overall level of FIT Integrity? . . . . %
(Do not estimate this. Simply add the five Constancies together and divide by 5 to get the average percentage.)

And finally, do you think you are depressed or anxious to any significant degree?

Anxiety   = Yes or No?
Depression = Yes or No?

Now you need to see whether your own self-perceptions match the actual levels by completing the *FIT Profiler*™. The *FIT Profiler*™ printed here is a short version of the real instrument that would be too complicated to self-score. Although the version here could not be reliably used when greater precision is needed (for example, if it is to be used in company selection processes, or as a training needs tool), it will provide a rough and ready picture which is good enough in this context. This will give you a good overall picture of yourself in terms of your:

- *Overall FITness*

- *Overall Behavioural Flexibility.* This is the measure that attempts to quantify the extent of your behavioural repertoire.

- *Your level of overall FIT Integrity.* Integrity is an overall computation based on your five Constancies.

- An assessment of each of the five *Constancies*:
  Self-responsibility
  Awareness/awakeness
  Balance
  Morality/ethics
  Fearlessness/self-assuredness

- *Your current levels of stress*, in terms of depression and general anxiety levels (this section is from a well-used measure developed by Professor Fletcher some years ago).

The *FIT Profiler*™ is designed to investigate various factors concerning you as a person, particularly in the way that you behave and think. If you would like a full assessment, which looks at a wider range of scores with a tool that has been developed with sophisticated statistical analysis, the authors can provide this.

When you fill in the short version of the *FIT Profiler*™ provided here it is important to remember that:

- All people are different. You should make sure you show how you feel personally and not how you think others see you, how you would like them to see you, or how you would like to see yourself.

- For your own sake, please answer all questions honestly.

- You need to answer all questions with your immediate feelings and not dwell too long on a particular question.

- Normally it is best to stick with your first reaction, but do feel free to change your answer if you wish.

The *FIT Profiler™* (Short version)

Section 1: *Thoughts and behaviour*

The FIT Profiler™ is concerned with how you might think and behave in any given circumstance. Please consider the following thoughts and behaviours and indicate the range that you might exhibit at any given time. This should be done in terms of what we call the comfort zone or the preferred zone. For example, you may do something under pressure from someone/something else that you would not ordinarily do and this may make you feel uncomfortable. If this is the case, you should not include it in your range.

Show the range of your thoughts and behaviours using the following examples as a guide.

Should you feel that you generally show your feelings freely, you might indicate this by showing a narrow range as in Example 1.

1. *Do you show your feelings freely* ⑤ *4 3 2 1 0 1 2 3 4 5*
   or keep them to yourself?   Show them   Neither one or   Keep them to
                                     freely   the other   yourself

Alternatively, you may feel that generally you are somewhere in the middle with the possibility of showing your feelings freely at times. In this case you might indicate this by showing a range as in Example 2.

2. *Do you show your feelings freely* ⑤ *4 3 2 1* ⓪ *1 2 3 4 5*
   or keep them to yourself?   Show them   Neither one or   Keep them to
                                     freely   the other   yourself

Another possibility is that you feel you shift between the middle point. If that is the case, you might indicate this in line with example 3.

3. *Do you show your feelings freely* *5 4 3 2* ① *0* ① *2 3 4 5*
   or keep them to yourself?   Show them   Neither one or   Keep them to
                                     freely   the other   yourself

You may show them freely at times and keep them to yourself at others. You might indicate this by showing the range in example 4.

4. Do you show your feelings freely
or keep them to yourself?

(5) 4 3 2 1 0 1 2 3 4 (5)

Show them   Neither one or   Keep them to
freely   the other   yourself

However, you may have no firm inclination yet err on showing your feelings sometimes. This
could be shown by reference to example 5.

5. Do you show your feelings freely
or keep them to yourself?

5 4 3 (2)(1) 0 1 2 3 4 5

Show them   Neither one or   Keep them to
freely   the other   yourself

You may indicate any range that you wish. But, remember that the range should only include
those thoughts and behaviours which feel comfortable to you and are by your own choosing.
If you understand, please continue.

1. Do you behave in a conventional
or unconventional manner?

5 4 3 (2) 1 0 1 2 (3) 4 5   V1

Conventional   Neither one or   Unconventional
     the other

2. Do you find yourself
daydreaming?

5 4 3 2 (1) 0 1 2 3 4 5   C1

Yes, all   Neither one or   No, not
the time   the other   at all

3. Would you consider yourself
to be a predictable person?

5 4 3 2 (1) 0 1 2 3 4 5   V2

Yes, very   Neither one or   No, very
predictable   the other   unpredictable

4. To what extent do you believe luck
contributes to your success?

5 4 3 2 (1) 0 1 2 3 4 5   C2

A large   Neither one or   A small
extent   the other   extent

5. When you are at work do
you wish you weren't?

5 4 (3) 2 1 0 1 2 (3) 4 5   C3

Yes, always   Neither one or   Never
     the other

6. Are you a reactive or
proactive person?

5 4 3 (2) 1 0 1 (2) 3 4 5   V3

Very   Neither one or   Very
reactive   the other   proactive

7. Do you meet difficult situations
head on or try to avoid them?

5 4 3 2 1 0 1 2 (3) 4 5   C4

Avoid   Neither one or   Head on
     the other

8. Do you believe you can change?

5 4 3 2 1 0 1 2 3 (4) 5   C5

No, not   Neither one or   Yes,
at all   the other   greatly

9. Are you group oriented or
individually centred?

5 4 (3) 2 1 0 1 2 (3) 4 5   V4

Very group   Neither one or   Very
oriented   the other   individually
     oriented

10. How important do you believe
it is to be alone?

5 4 3 2 1 0 1 2 (3) 4 5   C6

Not   Neither one or   Very
important   the other   important

11. Are you a risk taker or
a cautious person?

5 4 (3) 2 1 0 1 2 (3) 4 5   V5

Risk taking   Neither one or   Cautious
     the other

12. Are you always clear as to why you did something or are you often surprised with yourself?

5 4 3 2 1 0 1 2 (3) 4 5   C7
Often surprised ⋯ Neither one or the other ⋯ Always clear

13. Are you a single-minded or open-minded person?

5 4 3 2 1 0 1 2 3 (4) 5   V6   0
Single minded ⋯ Neither one or the other ⋯ Open minded

14. Do you have feelings of guilt about things you have said or done?

5 4 3 2 1 0 1 2 3 (4) 5   C8
Yes, always ⋯ Neither one or the other ⋯ No, never

15. When you are away from people you care about, do you miss them?

5 4 (3) 2 1 0 1 2 3 4 5   C9
Yes, always ⋯ Neither one or the other ⋯ No, never

16. When told someone's name, do you often forget it instantly?

5 4 3 (2) 1 0 1 2 3 4 5   C10
Yes, always ⋯ Neither one or the other ⋯ No, never

17. Do you feel that there is a fuzzy line between right and wrong?

5 4 3 2 1 0 1 2 3 4 (5)   C11
Yes, very fuzzy ⋯ Neither one or the other ⋯ No, not fuzzy

18. Are you a definite or flexible person?

5 4 3 2 1 0 1 2 3 4 (5)   V7   ✝
Very definite ⋯ Neither one or the other ⋯ Very flexible

19. Do you think that honesty is the best policy?

5 4 3 2 1 0 1 2 3 (4) 5   C12
No, never ⋯ Neither one or the other ⋯ Yes, always

20. Do fearful feelings stop you from doing many things?

5 4 3 (2) 1 0 1 2 3 4 5   C13
Yes, always ⋯ Neither one or the other ⋯ No, never

21. Would you consider doing something immoral or unethical if you could see a successful outcome?

5 4 3 2 1 0 1 2 3 (4) 5   C14
Yes, always ⋯ Neither one or the other ⋯ No, never

22. Does entering new situations and meeting new people worry you?

5 4 3 2 1 0 1 2 3 (4) 5   C15
Yes, always ⋯ Neither one or the other ⋯ No, never

The next short section is a simple self-assessment stress scale.

Section 2: *Thoughts and feelings*

Below are a number of statements that refer to thoughts and feelings. Consider each one in turn. Please say how often each one applies to you over the past few weeks, using one of the given categories, and write the appropriate number in the box to the right of the statement.

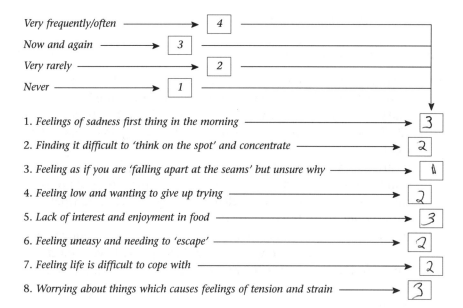

Very frequently/often ⟶ 4

Now and again ⟶ 3

Very rarely ⟶ 2

Never ⟶ 1

1. *Feelings of sadness first thing in the morning* ⟶ 3

2. *Finding it difficult to 'think on the spot' and concentrate* ⟶ 2

3. *Feeling as if you are 'falling apart at the seams' but unsure why* ⟶ 1

4. *Feeling low and wanting to give up trying* ⟶ 2

5. *Lack of interest and enjoyment in food* ⟶ 3

6. *Feeling uneasy and needing to 'escape'* ⟶ 2

7. *Feeling life is difficult to cope with* ⟶ 2

8. *Worrying about things which causes feelings of tension and strain* ⟶ 3

Analysing the *FIT Profiler*™

Section 1: *Thoughts and behaviours*

Behavioural range

To analyse your short *FIT Profiler*™ you need first to calculate the range of your responses for ten of the items. These items are those which are annotated with a 'V' at the right of the statement relating to the question. These are question numbers 1, 3, 6, 9, 11, 13 and 18.

Calculate the range using the guide below:

■   Count the number of spaces between the two circled numbers. If there is only one number circled this is scored as 0.

Example 1. (V Score = 8)   *Example 2. (V Score = 0)*

5 4 ③ 2   1   0   1   2   3   4 ⑤ V   5   4   3   2   1   0   1   2   3   4 ⑤ V

Each score should be a number between 0 and 10. Enter the numbers in the appropriate boxes in Table 5.1.

FIT Integrity and Constancy scores

This is a little more complicated and should be done with care:

1. First, identify the remaining items that are labelled C1–C15. These have to be scored according to an 11-point scale, scored from 0–10. The C questions are 2, 4, 5, 7, 8, 10, 12, 14, 15, 16, 17, 19, 20, 21 and 22. These have to be scored with a 0–10 scale going from left to right.

2. In the cases where you have indicated a range (i.e. circled two numbers) find out what the two circled numbers correspond to on the 0–10 scale. If you have circled just one number, note what that corresponds to on the 0–10 scale.

3. In the cases where you have circled two numbers simply add the two numbers together and divide by two. Where you have indicated a single number, that is the figure you need. All scores should be 10 or less.

4. Example 3:

   5 ④ 3 2 1 0 1 ② 3 4 5 C
   0 1 2 3 4 5 6 7 8 9 10

In example 3 the two circled numbers become 1 and 7. This makes 8. Divided by 2 this gives a final number of 4.

Now put the numbers you have obtained for each question in the corresponding box in Table 5.1 and add the totals in each of the columns to obtain the V, R, A, B, E and F totals. Be careful to locate the appropriate position on the grid. A misplaced score will result in an inaccurate profile.

Section 2: *Thoughts and feelings*

To analyse this section you simply add the numbers you have put in the response boxes:

> *Depression*: find your total for question numbers 1, 4, 5 and 7. This should be a number between 4 and 16. ||
> *Anxiety*: find your total for question numbers 2, 3, 6 and 8. This should be a number between 4 and 16.

TABLE 5.1

Question

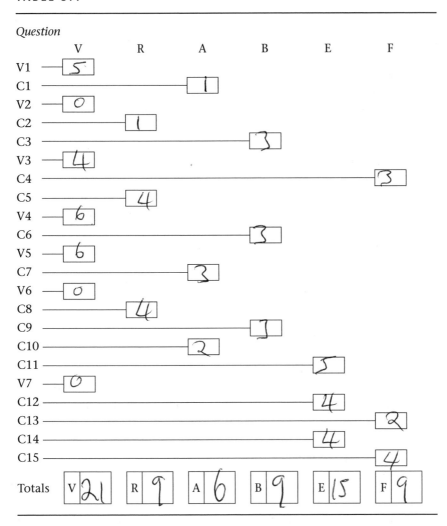

Question	V	R	A	B	E	F
V1	5					
C1			1			
V2	0					
C2		1				
C3				3		
V3	4					
C4						3
C5		4				
V4	6					
C6				3		
V5	6					
C7			3			
V6	0					
C8		4				
C9				1		
C10			2			
C11					5	
V7	0					
C12					4	
C13						2
C14					4	
C15						4
Totals	V 21	R 9	A 6	B 9	E 15	F 9

Analysing the various dimensions of the short *FIT Profiler*™

Section 1: *Thoughts and behaviour*

The full *FIT Profiler*™ can be analysed in many different ways. It also contains many more scores and more complex analyses than the short version for you to do here. This self-analysis will, however, give you a useful overall picture.

1. Calculating your Behavioural Flexibility (BFlex) score

   The BFlex score is a measure of how wide your behavioural repertoire is likely to be. It is useful to have a large repertoire because this gives you the necessary means to act appropriately across a wide variety of situations.

   To find out your BFlex score, simply multiply the V total in Table 5.1 by 10 and then divide the result by 7. This number will be between 0 and 100. Put the answer in the BFlex box in Table 5.2. Should you find that you have a zero BFlex score, insert a 1 in the BFlex box.

2. Calculating the Constancies scores

   Take each of the five Constancy scores (R for Self-responsibility; A for Awareness; B for Balance; E for Morality/Ethics; F for Fearlessness). Divide each of the R, A, B, E, F scores at the bottom of Table 5.1 by 3 and place each score in the relevant box in Table 5.2. The final numbers should each be 10 or less. They are likely to include a decimal point.

3. Calculating your FITness Integrity score

   Now calculate your FIT Integrity score by adding up each of your Constancy scores in Table 5.2 and multiply this number by 2. Be careful you do not add in the BFlex score too by mistake. The final number will be between 0 and 100. Round any decimal points to the closest whole number. This is your Integrity score. Write it in to Table 5.2.

4. Finding out your Overall FITness score

   Multiply your BFlex score by your Integrity score. Divide this number by 10. This is your overall FITness score. The final number will be 1000 or less.

TABLE 5.2 Your summary FITness scores

BFlex score	
Self-responsibility (R Score)	.
Awareness (A score)	.
Balance (B score)	.
Morality/ethics (E score)	.
Fearlessness (F score)	.
FIT Integrity	
Overall FITness Score	

What do the various FITness scores mean?

Overall FITness

The highest possible overall FITness score is 1000, although the majority of people score considerably less than this: often between one and two hundred. The overall FITness score does give you an indicator of the unfulfilled potential that you may not be utilizing. For example, a score of 450 – itself a very high score – would indicate that you still have untapped resources because you are only utilizing 45 percent of your FIT potential.

A score of less than 50 is very low, compared to the average. A score of 700 or more suggests a super-FITness that is very rare indeed. Any score over 400 is really very high; a score above 300 is also very good. Most people could aspire to raise their FITness scores to over 300. Scores in the range of 100–200 are the most commonly seen. A score lower than 150 shows considerable untapped potential that deserves serious consideration.

BFlex score

The BFlex score is an indicator of your FIT behavioural repertoire out of 100 (like a percentage score). If your score is as low as 20, for example, you have a very large potential as yet untapped. The larger the number the wider or greater your behavioural repertoire is likely to be, and the more chances you have of being able to act or decide to do the appropriate thing, rather than be guided only by your 'personality' and natural learned inclinations. Try to see why it is advantageous to have a large behavioural repertoire. You might like to look at your responses on the V-items and see how you think you could extend your behavioural range.

However, simply to extend the range of your behaviours is not enough. To behave appropriately requires the person to be aware of what makes a behaviour appropriate. This is why it is important to base behaviours and decisions on the components of FIT Integrity – the five Constancies. The Constancies are the drivers of behaviour in FIT theory, so to increase appropriate behaviour requires a consideration of the level of FIT Integrity.

FIT Integrity and the five Constancies

According to FIT theory, it is the level of the five Constancies that determine appropriateness of behaviour and your overall FIT Integrity.

The maximum score for each Constancy is 10. To have scored close to 10 in even one of the Constancies is unlikely although your goal should be to endeavour to get as close to the maximum as possible. A better target would be a score of between 8 and 9 – although this is itself a very high score. Scores of between 6 and 7 are quite common. Anything less than 5.5 is rather low and you should examine the reasons for this. The FIT Integrity score shows you what percentage capacity you are operating at.

Ideally, the scores on each of the Constancies should be roughly equal, although they are not usually. They should preferably be balanced at a high level (which would be equivalent to having a high FIT Integrity score). If you have any particularly low Constancy scores it is that area that needs to be looked at first. Do not work on your strengths, but on your weaknesses. Reflect on the level of your Constancy scores and the relations between them in the context of FIT theory and the points raised in Chapter 4.

Section 2: *Thoughts and feelings:*

In this section you should have two scores, one for the depression scale and one for general anxiety. The numbers should be between 4 and 16. If not, recheck your sums.

If you have scored between 4 and 11 (inclusive) on each of the scales, then your scores indicate levels that suggest you are not unduly anxious or depressed.

If you have scored 11 or 12 on either scale this means that you may have marginally high score(s) compared to others. It might be that both scores are at marginal levels, or just one. A marginally high score indicates a level high enough for you to take note. You should endeavour to change whatever it is that might be responsible for your depressed or anxious tendencies.

If you have scored from 13 to 16 on either scale, this suggests that you may be anxious or depressed to a significant level. This is something you should consider tackling, although you need to bear in mind that quite large numbers of ostensibly 'healthy' people will have similarly high levels. Our own research would indicate that about 10 percent of a healthy workforce would have levels this high. If you have a high score this will not be a suprise to you because you will not feel as positively as you might. You would doubtless prefer to feel better. FITness may help you in this regard, although it is not a tool that is designed to deal with clinical psychological problems.

For both the marginal and high scores you should try to determine what in your life is responsible for it. You might also want to take care to monitor how you feel and try to increase your decisions and behaviours that seem to make things better for you. We have found that FITter people have lower levels of depression and general anxiety. Perhaps the EXERcises in Chapter 6 might help.

Comparison of your initial estimations with *The FIT Profiler*™

Now that you have done both *The FIT Profiler*™ and your initial FIT estimations at the beginning of this chapter it will be interesting to compare them. Most people over-estimate their level of FITness and their Constancy levels. To directly compare the Constancy estimations with your Constancy scores derived from *The FIT Profiler*™ you need to divide the former percentage scores by 10 (or multiply the Profiler Constancy scores by 10).

Any mismatches in the estimations you have made may indicate the extent to which you have a distorted picture of yourself in terms of the FIT framework. In the next chapter we present some FIT EXERcises to help you to improve your *(Inner) FITness*™.

CHAPTER SIX

Personal FITness EXERcises

COMMITMENT

Until one is committed
there is hesitancy, the chance to draw back,
always ineffectiveness.
Concerning all acts of initiative (and creation)
there is one elementary truth,
the ignorance of which kills countless ideas
and splendid plans:
that the moment one definitely commits oneself,
then Providence moves too.
All sorts of things occur to help one that would
otherwise never have occurred.
A whole stream of events issue from the decision,
raising in one's favour all manner
of unforeseen incidents and meetings
and material assistance,
which no man could have dreamt
would come his way.

W. N. Murray

Aims of the FITness EXERcises

To enhance the likelihood that a person makes decisions according to FIT's five Constancies, rather than according to random or useless criteria.

To increase an individual's behavioural repertoire in any situation (this may require new behaviours as well as different uses of old ones).

To convert behavioural *variability* to behavioural *flexibility.*

To enhance personal skills and decrease personal vulnerability.

To make confidence, positiveness and felt efficacy outcomes of FITness (not a delusion or input to decisions).

The FIT EXERcises

The FIT EXERcises that follow will (if you wish) guide you in discovering various aspects about yourself in relation to FITness. The EXERcises are designed to assist you in reflecting on your behaviour and the various internal drivers that guide and motivate your behaviour. By doing the EXERcises you may discover elements of your behaviour or thinking that need to be modified or developed to achieve your FIT potential. Some people may set a ceiling on what they consider their potential – others may not. Different people will have different goals. It is important for you to be explicit about what you want in terms of your FIT development. You should ensure that a primary goal is to achieve at least two things:

- harmony or symmetry between the Constancies

and

- a high degree of Behavioural Flexibility.

You will need to be flexible about your goals and change them as you progress. You may even find that you change your goals so often that even your more global targets change. This may be because as you reach what you thought was an end state, other opportunities open themselves to you. These opportunities will need further personal development. The FIT EXERcises provide only an initial impetus for this development.

Many people misunderstand their potential and capabilities. Some strive too high. Others aim too low. Your goals need to be set in line with your ability and situation, although it is probably better to try to reach just a little bit further than not far enough. Hard goals, which you accept, are best. Reaching too far is a common mistake that can lead to consistent failure. So be realistic. The more you develop your potential, the easier it will be to accept and grow from failure. FITness development takes effort and time for most people, although a small idea can change an entire life without hard work. As with physical fitness, however, no-one else can make you FIT.

This chapter contains three FIT EXERcises:

- Awareness EXERcise

- Behavioural Flexibility EXERcise

- Balance EXERcise

These are designed to tackle and encompass some of the key aspects of *(Inner) FITness*™.

The Awareness EXERcise

The Awareness EXERcise is presented in a diary format. If you intend to do this over a period – for example, on a daily basis for a week or a month – you will need to find some way of recording your responses for the EXERcise many times.

The EXERcise asks you look back through your day and identify various aspects in relation to your level of Awareness. You are then given the opportunity to reflect on how you might change for the future. The ability to be aware is a major aspect of FITness – it is the engine of *(Inner) FITness*™. A high level of Awareness will eventually eradicate those automatic (habitual) thoughts and behaviours that have restricted your development in the past.

Always bear in mind the essential issue of balance between the Constancies. A high level of Awareness can be counterproductive if it is not matched with high levels in the other Constancies. You also need to achieve a balance between your 'inner' and 'external' Awareness. An elevated inner Awareness without a correspondingly high level of external Awareness can result in an over-focus on the self which promotes a lack of consideration for external aspects and situational demands. This will lead to inappropriate behaviour. An elevated external Awareness with a low inner Awareness can result in a person taking too much account of their environment and others, without taking sufficient account of the impact on themselves.

You should bear in mind that the Awareness EXERcise is restricted in a sense because it asks you to reflect on events that have happened. Awareness should be an ongoing activity and not take place after the event. However, EXERcises which interrupt daily living in a potentially intrusive manner were deemed too impractical for most people to do. Since Awareness is such an important aspect of *(Inner) FITness*™, however, we believe the Awareness EXERcise is a good first step.

The Behavioural Flexibility EXERcise

The Behavioural Flexibility EXERcise is designed to highlight the various behaviours that you actually have in your behavioural repertoire and the different ways you deploy them in different relationships. It is common for people to behave in different ways with different kinds of personal relationships. People generally restrict their behaviours to their comfort zone and this comfort zone varies with the different people you interact with. It is these comfort zones that the Behavioural Flexibility EXERcise aims to identify. Once you have identified your comfort zones you can then reflect on how they may be extended. Increasing Behavioural Flexibility is generally fairly simple to do. This is because it makes sense at a purely intuitive level. Behaving appropriately brings with it positive benefits. The aim of this EXERcise is to get you to use aspects of your own behavioural repertoire in circumstances where you may not have deployed them before. The next stage would be to enhance your actual behavioural repertoire. You can look at your own *FIT Profiler*™ results to provide some insights into where you might begin.

The Balance EXERcise

The Balance EXERcise concentrates on relationships with others, rather than just the balance you need to achieve in the various dimensions of your life. It asks you to consider your own view of the importance you give a relationship, the effort you put in to it, and the satisfaction you receive from it. The analysis then helps you to see whether or not these relationships are balanced, and gives pointers to what you might do to achieve a better balance between the three main scores.

Awareness EXERcise

The purpose of the following simple EXERcise is to help you to raise your Awareness, both to your internal and external world. The EXERcise takes the form of a diary. At the end of each working day you will be asked to reflect on the past 24 hours on various issues. Although simple in format you should think carefully about your answers.

Please take note that should you intend to continue this EXERcise over a period of time, you will need to copy the EXERcise beforehand.

These are the AIMS of the EXERcise:

Aim: Not to be on 'automatic pilot' but to think about what you are about to do or have just done or said. Also to think about what others are doing and saying. You have to become a constant analyser of yourself and your environment. The more you do this, the more potential you have to be FIT.

Aim: To analyse why the things that happen to you do so. To try to work out what your influence has been to cause these things.

Aim: To expand time to fit the work (not the other way round). Time passes quickly when you operate habitually, automatically, and without being aware. You can increase time, effectively, the more you are awake.

Aim: To learn to take heed of signals that you normally ignore or are not even aware of. To make the most of feedback you receive.

Awareness is monitoring and attending to your internal and external world.

Awareness is the engine of being FIT.

Date: ....

Respond to the following questions by ticking the relevant box. You should think about each question with regard to the past 24 HOURS.

Where there is a YES response, detail it in the box below the question.

	YES	NO
(a) Did you find yourself daydreaming today?	☐	☐

WHAT WAS IT ABOUT?

| *(b) On reflection did anything you do today have any negative repercussions of which you are only now aware?* | ☐ | ☐ |

WHAT WAS IT ?

| *(c) On reflection did anything anyone else do today have any negative repercussions of which you are only now aware?* | ☐ | ☐ |

WHAT WAS IT?

(d) Did anything surprise you today?

WHAT WAS IT?

YES   NO

(e) Did you forget an important piece of information today?

WHAT WAS IT?

(f) Did anything happen today that made you think your Awareness was low?

WHAT WAS IT?

(g) Would you have done anything differently, or better, had you been more aware?

WHAT WAS IT?

(h) Was any of your behaviour NOT appropriate to the situation?

Try to look at it from the point of view of others.

Remember Awareness is taking others into account as well as yourself.

WHICH BEHAVIOUR(S) IF ANY DO YOU NOW THINK WERE INAPPROPRIATE?

Did you answer YES to any of the above questions? If so, you now have the opportunity to reflect on the repercussions of your low Awareness.

You need to question yourself deeply as to why your Awareness was low.

Firstly look at the your Awareness level in relation to the other four Constancies.

YES   NO

(i)   Was there a correspondingly low level of Self-responsibility?

(j)   Was there a correspondingly low level of Fearlessness?

(k)   Was there a correspondingly low level of Balance?

(l)   Was there a correspondingly low level of Morality and Ethics?

Analysing your day

It is now time to analyse your day. You are only doing it now because you failed to do so at the time of the event. The following pointers may help you identify why your Awareness was low. Taking each item in turn, analyse all the instances where you ticked a YES.

As you analyse this EXERcise remember that a high level of Awareness is not useful on its own. Take, for example, someone with high Awareness but low levels of Fearlessness. Such a person may be aware of all the relevant signals from their inner and external worlds, but fear may prevent them from responding at all, or in an appropriate fashion. If you are awake the signals you receive, however subtle, are received fully and immediately. Your responses can also be complete and appropriate at the time.

If you did something today that you were not aware of, as it happened, you were asleep at the time. You need to understand why you were asleep. Were you thinking about totally unconnected issues? For example, thinking about home whilst at work or vice versa? Were you surprised by something? Did someone or thing make you jump? You need to discover WHY you were asleep or day dreaming, or what ever else you were doing. Were you just generally unhappy with the situation that you were in? If so, identify the reasons for your unhappiness. Low levels of one or all of the other Constancies often accompany a low state of Awareness. Whatever the reason for your low Awareness, the consequences will almost always be negative.

The importance of balance between the Constancies is paramount. All of the Constancies are inextricably linked with each other. Perhaps you could have avoided the problems or issues with greater Awareness by taking more account of other Constancies in guiding your behaviour or decisions.

In the case of a negative outcome it is usually much easier to rectify the situation immediately than it is later, especially if it deserves an apology or an immediate corrective action on your part. In the unFIT a low level of Morality and Ethics or Self-responsibility may prevent either immediate or later corrective action. The unFIT often fear error and possess an even greater fear of facing up to it. The FIT could be said to relish errors because they learn from them. Fear itself can also act to directly reduce the level of Awareness. Our perception of the world is narrowed down by fear to such an extent that people may not even be aware of making an error. The bad news for the unFIT is that everybody else probably knows.

A high level of Awareness will allow you to give an appropriate level of concentration to a detailed or complex problem. That is not all that is required, however. High levels of the other four Constancies will ensure that the outcome is personally and organizationally optimal. The FIT have the ability to concentrate but also possess the ability to switch between high demand tasks. Things of an irrelevant minor, or even quite major, matter that might compete for their attention and response would not distract the FIT individual.

Think about your general level of Awareness, as an integral part of your FIT Integrity. Ask yourself if today's events have made you consider doing something differently had you been given another chance. Do not simply dismiss the situation as a one-off. This is not learning. It is not FIT. You will probably do it again. It may even become a habit. A bad one. Operating with a low level of Awareness is like acting on automatic pilot with an eye on the past and not on the future. A low Awareness individual has to rely on what they know from the past. This is particularly relevant if you have identified an inappropriate behaviour. Maybe you committed an embarrassing act or spoke up when inappropriate or without sufficient thought. Maybe you should have spoken up and you didn't. FIT people always know how to behave and when to speak. The environment provides all the signals and as a chameleon the FIT adapts externally yet remains internally constant. They always act with FIT Integrity.

A high level of Awareness, together with high levels of the other Constancies, ensures that the FIT recognize the strengths and weakness of themselves and others. This means that they work within their own limitations.

Taking others for granted is associated with low Awareness. To be always aware is to be always learning. If something you have done whether inadvertently or not has unnecessarily troubled someone, it is still your responsibility. Remember that FITness is not always about there being a winner and a loser. In many situations there can often be a winner and a winner. Always be aware of the positive aspect. Even an error has a positive aspect if you have learned how not to do it next time. That is positive learning.

Do not restrict your Awareness training to the particular issues that have been presented above. Try to develop your Awareness in a more general or universal way. For example, when approaching someone in a corridor at work, don't bury your head in your papers. Look up, and acknowledge them in some way, even if you don't know them. If you do know them, it takes just a few seconds to say hello and no time to smile. Be especially attentive if it is a subordinate. For example, you might ask after their welfare with interest. Do not just pretend you are interested. Be aware. Don't ignore people just because you are busy. Paying attention and being aware of others is important whoever they are. It is important whoever you are too. Perhaps you could put aside a small amount of time each week or each day to be seen to be interested in others, particularly your subordinates. On a regular basis, as little as half an hour a week would do. Being awake to others is a very important aspect of FIT.

A sudden Awakeness by you may well raise suspicions as to why you are suddenly taking interest. This is something you will have to deal with. Deal with it in an honest manner. If you feel that this suspicion is a problem, particularly with your immediate subordinates and possibly your secretary, be honest. Admit that you used to be asleep but you have now woken up.

> People generally avoid reflection or awareness. The truth may be unearthed and the unFIT prefer the easy option. After all ignorance is bliss. Don't be ignorant.

This is your opportunity to reflect. Use the box below to say how much you might put it right tomorrow.

Behavioural Flexibility EXERcise

The purpose of the following EXERcise is to help you understand the importance of Behavioural Flexibility.

People take the path of least resistance (like river water). It is the structure of your behaviours and goals that determine what the path of least resistance is (like the riverbed). You can change the path (as an engineer can change the course of the riverbed). This will require engineering (and effort). Tackling problems without tackling the structure is bound to fail (positive thinking on its own will not do the job).

Our behaviours are very important, not only because of the effects they have on others (verbal and non-verbal behaviours), but because they provide our 'fingerprint' and our personal structures. These behaviours soon become 'automatic' in the sense that we do not cognitively heed or attend to what we say, do and behave. These 'behaviour habits' are the bane of FITness because they have outcomes for us without our noticing. Many of these outcomes will be negative because we have not properly engineered what we want and how we want to be. The negative effects will happen to us and to others with whom we interact.

There is a large degree of inertia against change and development that comes from our behaviour-habits. We need to learn to live with ambiguity, uncertainty, lack of invincibility, vulnerability, etc. These feelings are not necessarily uncomfortable ones – it is just the way you have learned to interpret them. Progress at a personal and organizational level comes from what we call the *uncertainty-enhancement effect*.

You must remember, however, that your behaviours also affect how you feel and perceive yourself, so changing your own behaviours can have a real impact on your own feelings and thoughts. Increasing your behavioural repertoire is a relatively simple issue but without a corresponding increase in your level of FIT Integrity it will not result in long-term success. This EXERcise will highlight the way you behave with different people. It is then up to you to reflect on whether your behaviour is appropriate. Appropriateness should be seen in terms of the effect on others but also the effect on you. It is of no value to increase your repertoire purely to suit others. It must have some gain for you. This is where the Constancies come into play.

The following FIT EXERcise is designed to investigate your ability to behave appropriately and flexibly in a number of relationships with different people:

- People you report to at work

- People who work for you/report to you

- Your spouse/partner

- Your close friends

- Your working acquaintances

- People you don't know

You might like to choose a different set of people appropriate to your own situation. Just change the labels on the EXERcise.

We have chosen just a few of the *FIT Profiler*™ behavioural dimensions, which are:

- Trusting/Cautious

- Energetic/Calm

- Extroverted/Introverted

- Proactive/Reactive

- Behave as wish/as expected

- Flexible/Definite

You may find it useful to extend or amend the EXERcise with different dimensions from the full *FIT Profiler*™.

> **Aim: to shift the certainty-uncertainty balance more towards Uncertainty Acceptance (of course, certainties are necessary in some areas).**

> **Aim: To behave appropriately in the situation – not to be restricted by your past. This will mean INCREASING the range of your behaviours.**

Behavioural Flexibility is ensuring that behaviour is always appropriate to the situation.

You may indicate any range of responses that you wish. But, remember that the range should only include those behaviours that feel comfortable to you and by your own choosing. Go back to Chapter 5 if you want to be reminded about how to make your answers. It is the same as used in the *FIT Profiler*™. The filling in of the shaded boxes will be explained later.

(1) PEOPLE YOU REPORT TO

*Please consider the way that you behave in your interactions
with the people you report to. In the first instance simply record
your behavioural range. Instructions will be given later to help you to
calculate the polarity and range figures.*

												Polarity		Range
												L	R	

(a) 5 4 3 2 1 0 1 2 3 4 5

    Very   Neither one or   Very
   trusting   the other   cautious

(b) 5 4 3 2 1 0 1 2 3 4 5

  Energetic   Neither one or   Calm
    driven   the other   relaxed

(c) 5 4 3 2 1 0 1 2 3 4 5

    Very   Neither one or   Very
  extroverted   the other   introverted

(d) 5 4 3 2 1 0 1 2 3 4 5

   Highly   Neither one or   Highly
  proactive   the other   reactive

(e) 5 4 3 2 1 0 1 2 3 4 5

  Behave as   Neither one or   Behave as
   I wish   the other   expected

(f) 5 4 3 2 1 0 1 2 3 4 5

   Very   Neither one or   Very
  flexible   the other   definite

(g) 5 4 3 2 1 0 1 2 3 4 5

   Very   Neither one or   Very
  assertive   the other   unassertive

(2) PEOPLE WHO WORK FOR YOU/REPORT TO YOU

Please consider the way that you behave in your interactions with the people who work for you/report to you. In the first instance simply record your behavioural range. Instructions will be given later to help you to calculate the polarity and range figures.

												Polarity	Range

(a) 5 4 3 2 1 0 1 2 3 4 5   L R

Very trusting — Neither one or the other — Very cautious

(b) 5 4 3 2 1 0 1 2 3 4 5

Energetic driven — Neither one or the other — Calm relaxed

(c) 5 4 3 2 1 0 1 2 3 4 5

Very extroverted — Neither one or the other — Very introverted

(d) 5 4 3 2 1 0 1 2 3 4 5

Highly proactive — Neither one or the other — Highly reactive

(e) 5 4 3 2 1 0 1 2 3 4 5

Behave as I wish — Neither one or the other — Behave as expected

(f) 5 4 3 2 1 0 1 2 3 4 5

Very flexible — Neither one or the other — Very definite

(g) 5 4 3 2 1 0 1 2 3 4 5

Very assertive — Neither one or the other — Very unassertive

(3) YOUR SPOUSE/PARTNER

*Please consider the way that you behave in your interactions
with your spouse/partner. In the first instance simply record
your behavioural range. Instructions will be given later to help you to
calculate the polarity and range figures.*

		Polarity	Range
		L R	

(a) 5   4   3   2   1   0   1   2   3   4   5

| Very trusting | Neither one or the other | Very cautious |

(b) 5   4   3   2   1   0   1   2   3   4   5

| Energetic driven | Neither one or the other | Calm relaxed |

(c) 5   4   3   2   1   0   1   2   3   4   5

| Very extroverted | Neither one or the other | Very introverted |

(d) 5   4   3   2   1   0   1   2   3   4   5

| Highly proactive | Neither one or the other | Highly reactive |

(e) 5   4   3   2   1   0   1   2   3   4   5

| Behave as I wish | Neither one or the other | Behave as expected |

(f) 5   4   3   2   1   0   1   2   3   4   5

| Very flexible | Neither one or the other | Very definite |

(g) 5   4   3   2   1   0   1   2   3   4   5

| Very assertive | Neither one or the other | Very unassertive |

(4) YOUR CLOSE FRIENDS

Please consider the way that you behave in your interactions
with your close friends. In the first instance simply record
your behavioural range. Instructions will be given later to help you to
calculate the polarity and range figures.

		Polarity	Range
		L R	

(a)   5   4   3   2   1   0   1   2   3   4   5

      Very   *Neither one or*   *Very*
     trusting   *the other*   *cautious*

(b)   5   4   3   2   1   0   1   2   3   4   5

    Energetic   *Neither one or*   *Calm*
     driven   *the other*   *relaxed*

(c)   5   4   3   2   1   0   1   2   3   4   5

     Very   *Neither one or*   *Very*
   extroverted   *the other*   *introverted*

(d)   5   4   3   2   1   0   1   2   3   4   5

    Highly   *Neither one or*   *Highly*
   proactive   *the other*   *reactive*

(e)   5   4   3   2   1   0   1   2   3   4   5

   Behave as   *Neither one or*   *Behave as*
    I wish   *the other*   *expected*

(f)   5   4   3   2   1   0   1   2   3   4   5

     Very   *Neither one or*   *Very*
    flexible   *the other*   *definite*

(g)   5   4   3   2   1   0   1   2   3   4   5

     Very   *Neither one or*   *Very*
   assertive   *the other*   *unassertive*

(5) YOUR WORKING ACQUAINTANCES

*Please consider the way that you behave in your interactions
with your working acquaintances. In the first instance simply record
your behavioural range. Instructions will be given later to help you to
calculate the polarity and range figures.*

		Polarity	Range
		L R	

(a)   5   4   3   2   1   0   1   2   3   4   5

Very   Neither one or   Very
trusting   the other   cautious

(b)   5   4   3   2   1   0   1   2   3   4   5

Energetic   Neither one or   Calm
driven   the other   relaxed

(c)   5   4   3   2   1   0   1   2   3   4   5

Very   Neither one or   Very
extroverted   the other   introverted

(d)   5   4   3   2   1   0   1   2   3   4   5

Highly   Neither one or   Highly
proactive   the other   reactive

(e)   5   4   3   2   1   0   1   2   3   4   5

Behave as   Neither one or   Behave as
I wish   the other   expected

(f)   5   4   3   2   1   0   1   2   3   4   5

Very   Neither one or   Very
flexible   the other   definite

(g)   5   4   3   2   1   0   1   2   3   4   5

Very   Neither one or   Very
assertive   the other   unassertive

(6) PEOPLE YOU DON'T KNOW

Please consider the way that you behave in your interactions with people you don't know. In the first instance simply record your behavioural range. Instructions will be given later to help you to calculate the polarity and range figures.

												Polarity	Range
												L R	
(a)	5	4	3	2	1	0	1	2	3	4	5		
	Very trusting				*Neither one or the other*				*Very cautious*				
(b)	5	4	3	2	1	0	1	2	3	4	5		
	Energetic driven				*Neither one or the other*				*Calm relaxed*				
(c)	5	4	3	2	1	0	1	2	3	4	5		
	Very extroverted				*Neither one or the other*				*Very introverted*				
(d)	5	4	3	2	1	0	1	2	3	4	5		
	Highly proactive				*Neither one or the other*				*Highly reactive*				
(e)	5	4	3	2	1	0	1	2	3	4	5		
	Behave as I wish				*Neither one or the other*				*Behave as expected*				
(f)	5	4	3	2	1	0	1	2	3	4	5		
	Very flexible				*Neither one or the other*				*Very definite*				
(g)	5	4	3	2	1	0	1	2	3	4	5		
	Very assertive				*Neither one or the other*				*Very unassertive*				

Scoring procedure

You now need to transcribe the data from the six relationships you have assessed on to the scoring grid overleaf.

* Behavioural range = the spread between your scores for any behaviour (if any).

* Polarity = when the score(s) do not span the '0' point, i.e. they are all to one end of the dimension.

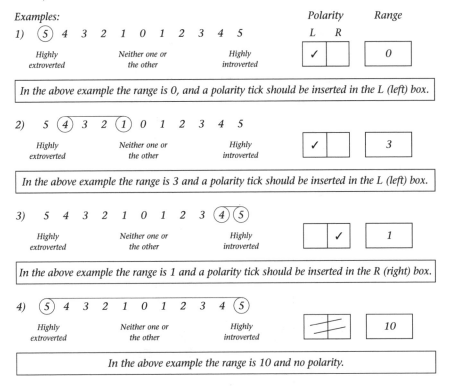

Examples:

1) (5) 4 3 2 1 0 1 2 3 4 5

Highly extroverted | Neither one or the other | Highly introverted

Polarity L R ✓ | Range 0

In the above example the range is 0, and a polarity tick should be inserted in the L (left) box.

2) 5 (4) 3 2 (1) 0 1 2 3 4 5

Highly extroverted | Neither one or the other | Highly introverted

✓ | 3

In the above example the range is 3 and a polarity tick should be inserted in the L (left) box.

3) 5 4 3 2 1 0 1 2 3 (4)(5)

Highly extroverted | Neither one or the other | Highly introverted

| ✓ | 1

In the above example the range is 1 and a polarity tick should be inserted in the R (right) box.

4) (5) 4 3 2 1 0 1 2 3 4 (5)

Highly extroverted | Neither one or the other | Highly introverted

10

In the above example the range is 10 and no polarity.

If you understand please fill in the shaded boxes in the EXERcise.

Once you have calculated both the range and polarity of each behaviour please copy them carefully on to the grid overleaf, taking care to ensure that each one is in its correct position.

Once this is done, add the individual ranges and insert the totals in the appropriate boxes (down and across).

Then assess how 'successful' you think that relationship is, for you and the other. The way you interpret or define 'success' is up to you – we do not want to constrain you by our own interpretation.

Score this success indicator on a 1–100 percent scale, where higher percentage scores are more successful.

Example

	Trusting Cautious		Energetic Calm		Extroverted Introverted		Proactive Reactive		Behave as wish or as expected		Flexible Definite		Assertive Unassertive		Total range	Success score
	Polarity L R	Range	Polarity L R	Range	Polarity L R	Range	Polarity L R	Range	Polarity L R	Range	Polarity L R	Range	Polarity L R	Range		
1. People you report to	✓	4	✓	3	✓	2	✓	5	✓	4	✓	2	✓	1	21	55%
2. People who report to you	✓	6														
3. Spouse/partner	┼┼	7														
4. Close friends	┼┼	8														
5. Acquaintances at work	✓	0														
6. People you don't know	✓	1														
Total dimension score		26														

This is a cross-section of what your grid should look like. For each behaviour and each relationship you should have entered a number in the range box (0–10) and a tick or blank in the polarity box. It is important that each piece of information is transcribed accurately as a slight mistake will provide you with a false picture.

	Trusting Cautious		Energetic Calm		Extroverted Introverted		Proactive Reactive		Behave as wish or as expected		Flexible Definite		Assertive Unassertive		Total range	Success score
	Polarity L R	Range	Polarity L R	Range	Polarity L R	Range	Polarity L R	Range	Polarity L R	Range	Polarity L R	Range	Polarity L R	Range		
1. People you report to																
2. People who report to you																
3. Spouse/partner																
4. Close friends																
5. Acquaintances at work																
6. People you don't know																
Total dimension range																

Analysing your level of Behavioural Flexibility

Now that you have transferred the information to the grid you have various aspects to consider:

- What is your level of overall Behavioural Flexibility?

- What is the level of Behavioural Flexibility within each relationship?

- What differences do you show in Behavioural Flexibility with different people?

- Is there a specific lack of flexibility in one or more of the behavioural dimensions?

- Is there a general tendency towards polarity of behaviour?

- Is there a polarity in one behavioural dimension but not in another?

- Is there a polarity in one relationship and an opposing polarity in other/another relationship/s?

- Is there any relationship between your various Behavioural Flexibility scores and the level of success you have indicated for each relationship?

- How does your Behavioural Flexibility in each relationship relate to your BFlex, FIT Integrity and Constancy scores in the *FIT Profiler*™ you completed (Chapter 5)?

In the first instance it is a valuable exercise to identify the total range indicators for both the individual dimensions and the individual relationships. In the case of the relationship (e.g. the person you report to) the optimum range score might be close to 70. In the case of the individual behavioural dimensions (e.g. trusting vs. cautious) the optimum score is probably nearer 60. How close are your scores to these? Do not be alarmed if your scores are a long way from the optimum. This is not unusual. First, look at the particular relationship ranges that have deflated your overall score. FITness requires that your behavioural repertoire should be at an optimal level for each relationship. That is to say that the behaviours that you employ with one individual are available for another. If you use a full repertoire with one individual, why should you feel a need to restrict your repertoire with another? Analyse why you do this.

In the same way, now look at the individual behavioural range scores. Which dimension(s) are deflating your overall range score? Are there behaviours that you utilize with one person and not another/

others? If you feel there is value in using the behaviours with one individual, why do you not do so with another?

You should also focus some attention on the Polarity indicators. For example, how many polar behaviours have you identified? FIT behaviour would show no polarity. Are there any opposing polarities when considering how you behave towards different people? If there are, this means you are behaving at one extreme of behaviour with one person and exactly the opposite way with another. If you accept the message that FIT offers, you may well see that this use of your behavioural repertoire is not effective. The essentials of Behavioural Flexibility are covered throughout this book and it is worth taking particular note of these areas.

It is common for people to behave in a particular way with one person and in a very different way with another. Often this difference is not appropriate or optimal for any party. It is also the case that people use different sets of behaviours in different environments. Some people plainly feel more comfortable in one kind of environment than they do in another and are likely to behave accordingly. This feeling of comfort may influence the way you behave with a particular person. It is this comfort feeling that is important to understand. The range of behaviours that people display in any behavioural dimension we have termed the 'comfort zone'. The comfort zone is likely to vary with different people. The EXERcise is therefore designed to identify your comfort zones and assist you in extending them.

As is evident from the example shown in Figure 6.1, the 'discomfort zone' (the light shaded area) is considerably larger than the 'comfort zone' (the black area). The position of the 'comfort zone' suggests that the person is generally unassertive when it comes to that behaviour with the

FIGURE 6.1 The assertiveness/unassertiveness 'comfort' and 'discomfort zone' for 'people you report to'

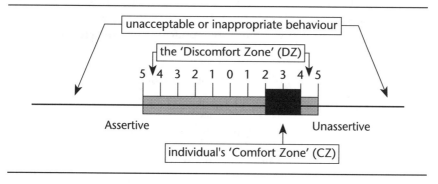

FIGURE 6.2 The assertiveness/unassertiveness 'comfort' and 'discomfort zone' for 'close friends'

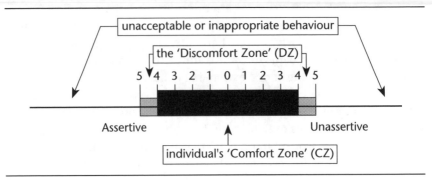

person that they report to. However, Figure 6.2 displays a totally different picture. With close friends there is significantly more flexibility. The individual shown here is much more likely to display both assertive and unassertive behaviour with close friends.

FIT states that what is possible in one relationship is possible in another. FIT also assumes that by increasing Behavioural Flexibility in all environments, people will enjoy visible and long-lasting benefits.

A major inhibitor to increasing behavioural flexibility is the feeling associated with the 'discomfort zone'. This feeling may range from mild distress to severe anxiety. The larger the 'discomfort zone' the greater likelihood of severe distress in certain circumstances.

Within the range of acceptable and appropriate behaviours, you need to *explore the DZ.*

Using the assertiveness/unassertiveness example above, it is likely that attempting to move into either extreme assertiveness or unasser-tiveness in the case of 'close friends' would not be too difficult, if it was appropriate. It may not even result in any mild concern. However, for the 'person you report to' relationship it may occasionally be necessary to be more assertive than you generally feel comfortable with. This may result in one of the following:

- Denial of the need to increase that behaviour

- Refusal to show that behaviour

- Showing that behaviour but wish you had not

- Exhibiting that behaviour and glad you did

It may be appropriate to now look at the relationship between your behavioural repertoire and the degree to which your behaviour is being appropriately guided by the five Constancies, just as you were asked to in the Awareness EXERcise. You may discover why there is a dissonance between the way you behave with one person and another. With regard to Awareness, if you are not awake you will not notice the often-subtle signals that show a change of behaviour is relevant or appropriate. It is likely that the Fearlessness and Self-responsibility Constancies also play a big part in restricting your behaviour. People often restrict their behaviour through a learning process that in the past has punished them for doing something other than what is expected of them. If we operate with a high level of FIT Integrity we do not need to be imprisoned or restricted in this way. Take the issue of gender differences, for example. It is generally accepted that males behave in a very different manner to females. Often the female is characterized as passive, calm, reactive and trusting. Males are often characterized by the opposite behaviours. People become conditioned during childhood by parents, teachers and peers. In business, the maleness traits have often been valued and the female traits being given little value. This view is now changing and the value of being able to have both types of behaviour in one's repertoire is now increasingly recognized. The FIT act with 'maleness' sometimes and 'femaleness' at other times. This is because at one time empathy, for example, may be highly appropriate but in another assertiveness is appropriate. It is this Behavioural Flexibility that promotes success in the FIT.

Fear is a major hurdle in extending our behavioural repertoire. Most people are happy and comfortable doing things in the way that they have done them in the past. Most people will continue along that same track and even be relatively successful in some aspects of their life. The FIT can identify the value of an extended repertoire, and are able to break through their fears to extend their comfort zones. The unFIT just want to be comfortable.

You have to take Responsibility yourself to decide to change and to try out the discomfort zone. Only by doing so can you extend your potential. You have to take Responsibility to speak up when necessary and to shut up when necessary.

In terms of Morality and Ethics we have a duty to treat others in a respectful and ethical manner. We need to regulate our behaviour in line with what is right and just. This may also require an enhanced behavioural repertoire.

The focus of this EXERcise has been on extending your behavioural repertoire in all relationships. It does not, of course, follow that all behaviours will be appropriate in every relationship. It is important, however, to increase your ability to display a wide repertoire of behaviour.

For example, it may never be appropriate to show assertive behaviour with a loved one but you should be able to if it were ever necessary.

When deciding on particular behavioural dimensions to enhance it is probably better to choose one in which you are exhibiting a polar behaviour. Choosing an already relatively flexible behaviour may be easier in some ways, but you may also find it more difficult to detect significant change – a feeling of success is often useful.

In doing the Behavioural EXERcise, or indeed any of the EXERcises, you do need to bear in mind that:

- Effort is needed.

- The short term and long term may be different.

- The aim is to become integrated so that what you do and what you want are symmetrical. By doing so, what will be will be designed by you.

- An increase in Behavioural Flexibility is of little value without a corresponding increase in the way behaviours and choices are guided by the Constancies. Without this, an increased behavioural repertoire may result in greater inappropriateness of behaviour.

It is important to note that our behavioural repertoire:

- was learned in the past;

- is often inappropriate for us and others with whom we interact;

- is often not relevant to our present situation;

- was learned from child-given templates but is for adult needs;

- impacts negatively on how we feel;

- impacts negatively on others and how we are perceived.

Finally, look at your success rating for each of the relationships. How high is it? Are they all 100 percent? If not, why not? The unFIT generally assume that life is just a roller-coaster of ups and downs. Not surprisingly, those who enjoy the highest highs also often suffer the lowest lows. The FIT decide that all dimensions of their lives should be 100 per cent successful. You might look at the link between your relationship-range scores and your own success score evaluations. Is there any relationship? Often a high success score accompanies a high range. This prompts the suggestion that increasing your behavioural repertoire may have an impact on the various success scores too.

Balance EXERcise

The purpose of the following EXERcise is to help you to effect a better balance between the important relationships in your life. Balance is concerned with how you manage the varied and diverse relationships in your life. It is concerned with the conscious and unconscious management of these relationships.

People often become imbalanced. For example, they become embroiled in only one dimension of their lives. This will have a detrimental effect on the other dimensions. For example, people who work too hard will often have problematic personal relationships, or difficult and less satisfying family lives.

Balance can be difficult to achieve for some because it requires people to reconsider the importance of each of the areas of their lives, their relationships, and the effort they put into them. These need to be in balance, although time spent in each area should not be taken as the determinant of importance. It is quality, not quantity, that Balance requires. People are often single-minded and over-focused, particularly in relationships. A new emotional attachment, for example, usually means a withdrawal from existing relationships, which is not balanced by any compensating attention. The maintenance of these existing relationships can, therefore, become a problem, particularly in the short term. While you are in a particular situation, relationship, or doing something you should consider it of the highest importance and put the maximum effort in. No longer will you struggle to go to work with a feeling of foreboding. No longer will you stay unnecessarily late at the office. It is likely that your time management skills will improve. The FIT do not look forward to leaving a particular part of their lives, they merely look forward to going to another. The unFIT, on the contrary, often prefer to be where they feel comfortable with limited awareness of the rest of the world. The ability to Balance your life means that you would no longer feel the emotional pain of leaving but elation for where you are going. This does not imply, however, any lack of attachment or dedication to anyone or anything. The FIT are attached to all the dimensions of their lives. The unFIT often have a single passion, the FIT many. A highly Balanced individual reaps the rewards of bringing the richness and knowledge to other relationships. This is another positive attribute of Balance.

When doing the Balance EXERcise, you may consider some of the relationships in the EXERcise as being unimportant. You should, however, attempt to complete the whole EXERcise. There may be relationships in your life that you consider important which do not in fact appear. For example, a family pet or such like may have tremendous importance to you personally. Feel free to add that relationship and score it in exactly the same manner as the others.

You will also be asked to give ratings to the relationship with yourself. Do not dismiss this aspect. It is the most important. We believe that the better the relationship you have with yourself, the better your external relationships will be. Respect for others is very important, but so is self-respect. External and internal relationships require consideration in the Balance Constancy.

The Balance EXERcise asks you to indicate how you feel and how you think about others in terms of four aspects:

- The *importance* of the relationship to you.

- The amount of *effort* you put into the relationship, and your perception of the amount of effort the other person puts into it. Again ask the other if you wish.

- The level of *satisfaction* you feel with the relationship, followed by your perception of the other person's level of satisfaction. In the same way, feel free to ask the other.

- Your perception of the *other person's* view. If you wish you may actually ask the other party for their opinion. This would result in a considerably more objective measure. But be sure you are ready and able to receive their answer, and especially that it may be different from what you were expecting to hear.

Do not confuse satisfaction, effort or importance with the amount of time spent in the relationship. A brief moment can be as important to you as things that take a good deal of time.

> **Aim: To balance and integrate each facet of each relationship and between each relationship in your life. That is to say that each part of your life receives the due care and attention that it merits.**

> **Aim: To achieve a harmony, balance and symmetry between the central spheres of your life. This will include inner balance (closeness of elements to your personal hub) as well as balance between the external elements (e.g. home and work).**

> **Balance is making sure each part of your life receives due care and attention. If you consider the important parts important put sufficient effort into them and receive sufficient satisfaction from them.**

(1) IMPORTANCE

Please consider the following RELATIONSHIPS and rate them out of 10 with regard to how IMPORTANT you and the other see them.

1 = Low importance   10 = High importance

Remember, do not confuse IMPORTANCE with time.

	You	Other	misFIT
PEOPLE YOU REPORT TO			
(a) How important do you regard this relationship?			
(a) How important do you think they regard it?			
PEOPLE WHO REPORT TO YOU			
(b) How important do you regard this relationship?			
(b) How important do you think they regard it?			
YOUR SPOUSE/PARTNER			
(c) How important do you regard this relationship?			
(c) How important do you think they regard it?			
YOUR CLOSE FRIENDS			
(d) How important do you regard this relationship?			
(d) How important do you think they regard it?			
YOUR WORKING ACQUAINTANCES			
(e) How important do you regard this relationship?			
(e) How important do you think they regard it?			
PEOPLE YOU DON'T KNOW			
(f) How important do you regard this relationship?			
(f) How important do you think they regard it?			
YOURSELF			
(g) How important do you regard this relationship?			
(g) How important you should regard it?		10	

Now calculate the misFIT scores by subtracting the lower score from the higher score and placing it in the misFIT boxes. This will give you an indication of the misFIT if any between your idea of importance and that of the other person. Now transfer the 'you' and 'other' scores onto the grid on page 98.

(2) EFFORT/FOCUS

Please consider the following RELATIONSHIPS and rate them out of 10 with regard to how much EFFORT/FOCUS *you and the other put into the relationship.*

1 = Low effort/focus   10 = High effort/focus

Remember, do not confuse EFFORT/FOCUS *with time spent.*

	You	*Other*	*misFIT*
PEOPLE YOU REPORT TO			
(a) How much effort/focus do you put into the relationship?			
(a) How much effort/focus do you think they put into it?			
PEOPLE WHO REPORT TO YOU			
(b) How much effort/focus do you put into the relationship?			
(b) How much effort/focus do you think they put into it?			
YOUR SPOUSE/PARTNER			
(c) How much effort/focus do you put into the relationship?			
(c) How much effort/focus do you think they put into it?			
YOUR CLOSE FRIENDS			
(d) How much effort/focus do you put into the relationship?			
(d) How much effort/focus do you think they put into it?			
YOUR WORKING ACQUAINTANCES			
(e) How much effort/focus do you put into the relationship?			
(e) How much effort/focus do you think they put into it?			
PEOPLE YOU DON'T KNOW			
(f) How much effort/focus do you put into the relationship?			
(f) How much effort/focus do you think they put into it?			
YOURSELF			
(g) How much effort/focus do you put into the relationship?			
(g) How much effort/focus you should put into it?	10		

Now calculate the misFIT scores by subtracting the lower score from the higher score and placing it in the misFIT boxes. This will give you an indication of the misFIT if any between your idea of effort/focus put in by you and that of the other person. Now transfer the 'you' and 'other' scores onto the grid on page 98.

(3) SATISFACTION

*Please consider the following RELATIONSHIPS and rate them out of 10 with
regard to how much SATISFACTION you and the other have with the relationship.*

1 = Low satisfaction   10 = High satsifaction

Remember, do not confuse SATISFACTION with time spent.

	You	Other	misFIT
PEOPLE YOU REPORT TO			
(a) How satisfied are you with this relationship?			
(a) How satisfied do you think they are?			
PEOPLE WHO REPORT TO YOU			
(b) How satisfied are you with this relationship?			
(b) How satisfied do you think they are?			
YOUR SPOUSE/PARTNER			
(c) How satisfied are you with this relationship?			
(c) How satisfied do you think they are?			
YOUR CLOSE FRIENDS			
(d) How satisfied are you with this relationship?			
(d) How satisfied do you think they are?			
YOUR WORKING ACQUAINTANCES			
(e) How satisfied are you with this relationship?			
(e) How satisfied do you think they are?			
PEOPLE YOU DON'T KNOW			
(f) How satisfied are you with this relationship?			
(f) How satisfied do you think they are?			
YOURSELF			
(g) How satisfied are you with this relationship?			
(g) How satisfied you should be with this relationship?	10		

*Now calculate the misFIT scores by subtracting the lower score from the higher score and
placing it in the misFIT boxes. This will give you an indication of the misFIT if any between
your idea of satisfaction and that of the other person. Now transfer the 'you' and 'other' scores
onto the grid on page 98.*

The purpose of the balance EXERcise is to show three things:

- The Balance or FIT that you have within a particular relationship. For example, is there a misFIT between satisfaction, effort and importance?

- The Balance between all your relationships. For example, do you hold a higher regard for one relationship than one or all others?

- Your perception (or theirs) of how others see their relationship with you. For example, is there a misFIT between your perceptions and those of the other?

	Importance to you	Effort/focus by you	Satisfaction to you	Total You	Importance to the other	Effort/focus by the other	Satisfaction to the other	Total Other
People you report to								
People who report to you								
Your spouse/partner								
Your close friends								
Your working acquaintances								
People you don't know								
Yourself								

Analysing the Balance EXERcise

Before starting on the interpretation of your Balance EXERcise it is important to remember that a long-term benefit in your level of Balance can only be achieved with a firm understanding of FIT Integrity. That is to say that you do it with full consideration of the other Constancies. For example, only with Awareness will you recognize the internal and external factors that are affecting your level of Balance. Do you need to change or does the other person need to? Only with Responsibility do we truly recognize our role in the relationship. Balance must be achieved within a Moral and Ethical framework. And last but not least is Fearlessness. It will take great courage sometimes to effect change. It is easier in the short term to avoid the problems and therefore not even consider change. All strategies which do not involve all aspects of FIT Integrity may result in short-term benefits but rarely will these benefits serve you in the long term.

The EXERcise should be interpreted in two parts:

■   First, in terms of the overall position. Look at each relationship in turn and carefully inspect the scores in terms of the degree of FIT or Balance.

■   If there is a misFIT or lack of Balance return to the EXERcise and inspect the individual misFIT scores.

You now need to look at the specific aspects of the balance EXERcise.

Remember that the degree of FIT is a crucial factor. For example, if all scores within a particular relationship are low it is unlikely to be of concern. However, you might question why you have scored it so low. If a relationship scores very low you should try to analyse and understand what is going wrong. It could be that the relationship truly does not deserve to be rated as important or a high degree of effort put into it. It may, however, be important to the other person. If this is the case you have a responsibility to the other to communicate your feelings. The relationship may need to be re-assessed and you should consider what will increase the individual and overall scores, even if that means considering a job move, or greater distancing from a relationship. According to FIT, having relationships that are unbalanced or low scoring is not in the interests of either party in the longer term. Some pointers are given below that may assist you in identifying possible factors that are diminishing your Balance potential. Note, however, that each person's level of Balance will be very different and so it is up to you to determine what is appropriate for you.

Good initial indicators of Balance in a particular relationship are the total 'you' and 'other' scores in columns 3 and 6 on page 98. The nearer they are to 30 the less likely they have been, or will be, problematic. So, in the first instance, concentrate on the lower totals for each individual relationship in terms of how you see it. However, it may be that the 'others' score is very different from the 'you' total. Assess it in terms of how you see it in relation to how the other sees it. Those relationships that are likely to be causing concern or likely to in the future are the relationships that are low in individual, or overall scores, or those that display a misfit between the 'you' and 'other' scores.

Pointers to consider:

- Is there a FIT or balance between *your* levels of importance, satisfaction and effort/focus and your perception of the *'other'*?

- Do you feel that the relationship is two-way? In other words, is your level of importance/satisfaction/effort matched by the other's level?

- Is there a FIT or balance between the level of importance and effort, and the degree of satisfaction you feel?

- Is there a FIT or balance between the level of importance and effort, and the degree of satisfaction you feel the other person has?

- It is important to consider the 'other's' view because it may well be that your own input into the relationship is too great. It may be that the best way to achieve balance is for the other party to increase *their* input. Of course this is not easy to bring about, may not be appropriate, or may not be possible (for example, they may wish to increase their input but lack the skills to do so). A basic premise of FIT is that we should concentrate on our own FITness and not on seeing others as responsible for a problem, or trying to change others. We do, however, possess the ability to change our responses to others which will affect their perceptions and behaviours.

Improving your understanding of your scores:

If the score for any one element (i.e. importance, effort, satisfaction) is higher or lower than one or both of the other scores:

- Have you an inflated regard for this relationship? Or, alternatively, should it be given greater or less emphasis?

- Do you regard this relationship as being more important than the other party?

- Is it time to re-assess the level of importance that you place on this relationship?

- If the satisfaction score is lower than one or both of the other two scores:
  - Are you putting too much effort into the relationship or do you feel that the other party is not putting enough effort into it?
  - Are you demanding too much? Or too little?
  - Would you prefer more demands to be put on you?
  - Are you expecting too much?
  - Do you feel that you do not meet the demands or expectations made by the other party? Or too little?
  - Are you putting too much effort into the relationship? Is the other party making enough effort?

There are many such questions. Try to consider what other issues you could raise. In the table on page 98 you calculated the 'Total to you' score and a 'Total other' score for each of the relationships (people).

It should be a goal, however unrealistic, to strive for a score of 30 in each relationship. If this is not possible in the short term, at least identify the areas responsible for the deficiency and aim for a FIT between the scores on satisfaction, effort/focus and importance.

In order to achieve Balance, enhanced Behavioural Flexibility, or indeed to achieve any development in terms of FITness, requires that you plan what to do to change from the current state of affairs. For some, this planning process will come naturally. Others may need to be more systematic. Planning for success is worth that effort. We finish this chapter by leaving you with some issues you might wish to consider when making plans and changes. For us, the principal issue to consider is whether or not the planned actions and decisions are informed sufficiently by the five FITness Constancies. In other words, will they be carried out with Integrity? Below are some aspects you might like to consider when trying to change the way you have done things. We have concentrated on the five Constancies since these are the inner building blocks for FITness.

Fearlessness:

- Are the planned changes personally stretching? Are mistakes, errors or failure a possibility? They should be. The FIT are prepared to make mistakes and learn from them. Alternatively, are the plans easily achievable and not personally stretching? Make them so.

- Are you happy to deal with criticism if it goes wrong? You will need to be ready for issues to arise.

- Fear can get in the way of change and improvement. You will need to try to decide and act fearlessly if you are to do what is right and appropriate.

- Are you prepared to step out of your 'comfort zone' and experience some discomfort? This may be necessary.

- Are you taking a new, or novel, or even unconventional approach? Maybe one is needed to break your past habits.

Balance:

- Can you achieve a balance with what you know and what you need to learn? If not, do something to make sure you cover this aspect.

- Can you achieve a balance between the life dimensions that are relevant to you (work, home and self?) without over-focusing?

Self-responsibility:

- Are you ready to take personal responsibility for the success or failure of your plans? If not, work on this first. No one else, or nothing else, should figure in the blaming stakes.

- Does your plan rely to any degree on lucky breaks, or being in the right place at the right time? If so, rethink and eradicate that 'luck' element.

Morals/Ethics:

- Does your plan morally/ethically compromise you or anybody else involved with it?

- Have you taken account of the possible cost to others?

Awareness/Awakeness:

- Have you thought about the kinds of feedback that you will need to be aware of to effect planned changes?

- Are you prepared to put in the extra effort needed to enhance your Awareness levels to bring about what you want?

FIGURE 6.3   A skeleton flow-chart for personal change

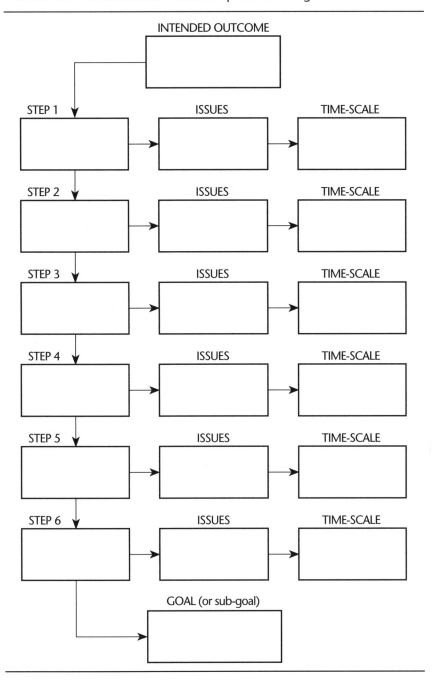

You might find it useful to plot your intentions and plans on the flow chart in Figure 6.3. Initially you could use this to chart the route to achieving a better Balance – paying attention to the results of the Balance EXERcise so far. Later, you may consider broader FIT issues. In the boxes labelled 'issues' you should ensure that you interrogate your intentions in terms of the Constancies, as well as other aspects you see as important to the context. The different steps should lead to the 'goal' (which may be a sub-goal that goes some way towards a higher goal). Of course, you may need to write down more steps, or have several pages that lead towards the desired outcome by a more circuitous route, with various smaller planned steps. For example, you might start with the intended outcome of giving more consideration to your spouse or partner (with the end goal of having a better relationship). Step 1 might be to think about the ways in which you do not show consideration and the ways you could. Issues might be that you both bicker, you are stressed at work, or you don't have time. The issues might be more fundamental – for example, about the ways in which you are, or are not, compatible. You might give this Step 1 three days. Step 2 might be to think about your partner's perceptions and state. Issues could be that they don't realize that you are stressed, or they are stressed and busy too. This might take one day. Step 3 might be to monitor and mutually identify the issues as they arise – for example, to communicate more – and to do this for a few days or a week. Then Step 4 could be the first step towards really trying to make changes. And so on.

You can use this example to help you plan and to start to make some changes in your life. Most people allow things to happen without ever challenging why. Generally people do not engage in the 'why' because they fear the consequences. Take that first step and try to chart a solution to issues you have. This will itself probably help. You may then find that change is not as difficult as you thought. Do it!

■ CHAPTER SEVEN ■

The Constancies

In *Escape Attempts: The Theory and Practice of Resistance to Everyday Life* by Professors Stanley Cohen and Laurie Taylor, the authors describe how human beings are generally dissatisfied with their picture of everyday reality and the psychological strategies they adopt for ignoring it, distorting it and subverting it: their escape attempts. These attempts include developing a different self-identity, periodically resorting to self-awareness, role distancing (doing things but seeing ourselves as acting them out, not owning them), script evasion (or looking at things differently), fantasy or free areas (e.g. activities, hobbies, cultural pursuits, drugs). In the main these different strategies do not work in the longer term but serve to 'nudge away our sense of reality and its routines for a short time' (p. 170). They go on to say that sometimes, for some people, their model of reality slips away – they experience 'reality slips' or 'momentary slips through the fabric' – what William James called 'unaccountable invasive alterations of consciousness' (*Varieties of Religious Experience*, Fontana, 1960, p. 236). These reality slips are usually viewed from a religious perspective (if they persist) and profoundly change the way the person looks at the world. We do not share the view that religion constitutes a reality slip because we see such experiences as the consequence of hidden and unrequited psychological needs. However, it is our view that FIT can, for some, offer a tool to prise out a different reality and one that can provide a *modus operandi* 'by which a self hitherto divided and consciously wrong, inferior and unhappy, becomes unified and consciously right, superior and happy' (James, *op cit.*, p. 194).

FITness does require an integration of the emotional and the rational demands of living and it is the five Constancies that provide the bedrock of this integration: the basis and constituents of FIT Integrity. It is these Constancies that we consider in more detail in this chapter. We look, in particular, at each Constancy in turn and then consider one special topic that we believe is related closely to the Constancy. In choosing these topics we have tried to take issues that are central or important aspects with wide currency.

However, before launching on that journey, we thought it useful to introduce a topic that is central to being FIT or developing FITness: being self-aware and involved, yet detached enough to rationally analyse a situation in terms of the Constancies. This has been called 'detached involvement'.

Detached involvement

The integration of apparent opposites, and of head and heart, and of emotion and reason is necessary for self-development. 'Detached involvement' is a demonstration of this development. To be FIT is to be able to make decisions and behave with a detached involvement. Operating with detached involvement requires a vision-driven self-management, which the FIT perspective involves.

Dr Jagdish Parikh, in a book entitled *Managing Your Self: Management by Detached Involvement* published in 1991, advocates the integration of objectivity in decisions and actions with self-management at each of his five levels (society, organization, manager, person, existential being). The extent to which we are able to integrate or 'fit' the external demands with our inner needs, the more successful and healthy we become:

> showing that the centre of your being is a constant, strong, and stable pivot of consciousness, a base which liberates you into greater activity: 'doing more' and at the same time feeling steady and secure and, therefore, 'feeling better'. This in turn facilitates and triggers even more activity and higher performance. The centred consciousness, or central pivot, is the perennial source of positive energy – much like the eye of the storm, which is a kind of silent, dynamic vacuum but is a source of all the energy in the storm. (Parikh, 1991, pp. 146–150)

In essence, detached involvement is achieved by an involvement 'in the activities of your work and life, in your efforts to be successful, but you should remain detached from the activities or rewards themselves' (Parikh, 1991, p. xiv).

Management by detached involvement integrates what we have to do with what we like to do. In the work context, this can be very beneficial. Dr Parikh goes on to say:

'It is only when you operate from a detached consciousness that you can bring about authentic organizational transformation. In the process you will be transforming organizational cultures from hierarchical structures into mutual support networks, from management styles based on control and aggression to those oriented toward caring and connection. Moreover, in the final analysis, you will be transforming your role from that of either innocent or professional to that of master manager.' (p. xvi)

Thus, this self-mastery ripples outwards to all areas in which we become involved. It also determines how the inner self copes with the many potential conflicts and issues which cause dissonance and the silent erosion of our inner strength. That is why we must try to remain vigilant to the factors that influence our decisions and behaviours and take personal charge over them. To be able to manage this means making the most of the feedback we receive from our environment and others – which often goes unnoticed – and this can only happen effectively when we are awake and aware of it.

Awareness/awakeness

Awareness is an important Constancy because it is central to the functioning of the other four. But by awareness we do not mean either 'self-awareness' with its many connotations, or consciousness. These are different concepts, albeit with their links to what we mean by awareness. In Chapter 2 we defined the awareness Constancy as:

the degree to which an individual monitors and attends to their internal and external worlds

Central to the notion of all the Constancies in FIT, however, is the active conscious consideration of information, personal or environmental, internal or external, in order to inform decision or action choices. This is Awareness/awakeness. Consciousness can have a quite passive meaning relating to some kind of internal personal experience. For us awareness is an active process with a goal that sits outside the experience itself. It is our contention that many people who are conscious are hardly ever aware and awake in the FITness sense. Most people are asleep with their eyes open.

Special topic – self-monitoring and self-regulation

One aspect of FITness is that the FIT individual monitors themselves in relation to the demands of the environment, in order to determine appropriate behaviour. One prediction of FIT, therefore, would be that those who have a more developed ability for self-monitoring – those who have a more clearly distinguished identity which is independent of their public personas – should also show a greater behavioural repertoire than those with a less developed ability. This is because they will not be as chained to their learned behaviour patterns. Mark Snyder (1987) has researched the psychology of self-monitoring in a book called *Public Appearances/Private Realities*. Snyder says that those who are more aware of the need to distinguish between their public face and their internal image of themselves are 'high self-monitors'. High self-monitors are good managers of the impression they give of themselves to others and have as many social selves as they have social settings. High self-monitors can be seen as actors who behave in a way that is contingent upon the situation, and have learned the skills to do this in a convincing way; they are social chameleons. Low self-monitors, however, do not have these 'acting' or social presentation skills. They do not change the way they are depending upon the situation, and will behave more firmly in accordance to their inner self-image and true beliefs.

Snyder sees high self-monitors as having more control over their non-verbal expressive behaviours; they have greater sensitivity to situational cues which can guide appropriate behaviour; they are better at reading situations and people and do not get seduced by face-value; they have greater gaps or inconsistencies between their attitudes and behaviours, they will act apparently more inconsistently and so it is more difficult to predict their behaviour; they have a much broader social matrix with greater segmentation or non-overlapping groups of friends; they are more concerned with physical appearance than with personal attributes in initiating close relationships; appear less committed in relationships; have more serial partners, including marriages; and perform better in work situations where they can use their social skills. Self-monitoring style does not show any relationship with the incidence of depression. Snyder sees the 'lives of high self-monitors appear to be meaningful reflections of a pragmatic sense of self; those of low self-monitors reflect a principled sense of self' (1987, p. 190).

High self-monitors would, on the face of it, have some common-alities with FIT personalities – both are flexible, responsive and adaptable, have or develop good social skills and have more flexible and apparently unpredictable behaviour. However, there are crucial differences between the FIT and the high self-monitors: the latter could be said to be deceivers, or impression managers, perhaps without obvious principles. Although Snyder suggests that when evaluated against the standards of their own definitions of the self, they are very much in possession of themselves, and are not to be considered Machiavellians who used exploitative techniques. The FIT are quite different – their self-base is very powerful, and not shallow, and they have a very sound inner core (Integrity). There is no sense in which they should be seen as just activity based – a criticism of the high self-monitors – since their activities are firmly based on the inner five Constancies which define their real integrity.

Fearlessness

In her book *Beyond Fear*, Barbara Rowe (1987) says 'Fear, like death, is the great unmentionable' (p. 19) which grows up with us as we get older and then, when we are adult, hides its reasons from us which had their place in our childhood experiences. As adults, however, we have the capacities to understand and reason. As adults we should learn to develop less, rather than more, fear. This we are rarely encouraged to do. On the contrary, our adult life is spent saving fear and investing heavily in it. Generally speaking we are not talking about fear in the useful sense as that feeling which saves us from physical dangers (a man with a gun, or a dangerous animal from which we should run). That type of defence for fear is often proposed by a strong pro-fear lobby. Fear in our sense – the mind-trapping, usually self-inflicted, fear of living – not fear of fearful things – has no value except to counsellors and psychologists and the pharmaceutical industry. As humans in a relatively civilized society we are rarely in need of exercising a decision of 'fight or flight'. That time has largely gone and is useful for the animals of the jungle. Fearlessness, not fear, has value in the human jungle. If one could develop a mastery of appropriate fearlessness, one would indeed do well in that jungle.

Rowe sees life as charting a course between an array of 'unavoidable conflicts', including:

Being an individual and ignoring the demands of others, to subsuming these individual needs to being a member of a group and getting those benefits.

Regarding yourself as having no value or worth and being imperfect, to regarding yourself as completely valuable and perfect.

From the moment of birth we have to decide between the conflicts of freedom and security ('Freedom's just another word for nothing left to lose')

and having an infinite choice, to having no choice at all,

and not being responsible for anything to being totally responsible for everything,

and being social we must choose a point between the risk of rejection and the risk of loneliness.

In these life equations our fear level usually decides for us. We create fear-brick barriers with which to circumscribe and defend ourselves. Our fears build us and define us. They create the 'individual' that is you. And the 'you' defends that position with great personal force. What a waste of potentially useful energy!

But fear is a great dictator that takes away choice and decision from the individual. As scientists have discovered, it is the foundation of many disorders and illnesses. Professor Stanley Rachman in his book *The Meanings of Fear* published in 1974 wrote that 'Fear, or its first cousin, anxiety, plays a major part in most neurotic disorders ... we are left with psychological methods for reducing fears' (p. 15).

Development of the Fearlessness Constancy returns emphasis to personal decision making as the shaper of well-being and growth. The fearless person, when acting in concert with the other Constancies, will chart an appropriate course through Rowe's 'unavoidable conflicts'. For the FIT person these are not in conflict at all: appropriateness and contextual need will require different responses in different circumstances.

Fear is sometimes viewed by commentators and scientists of human behaviour as a good thing which provides a safety net for the individual lest they stray into dangerous territory. It has also been seen as having value in helping people adapt or cope with impending difficulties and dangers and to play a positive role in getting people to be more aware in combat, or to take hygiene precautions, or to make them stop smoking. This position is understandable but presents a position that is an abrogation of personal responsibility. Such a position has some force for the young and those who cannot yet think for themselves. It is an insult to the individual: making automatic responses without understanding why, or even attempting to, is an instinctive, biological animal reaction, not that of a contemplative mature adult. Human beings should learn to develop their humanness which means learning to benefit from fearlessness (adequately checked by the other Constancies) and taking responsibility and advantage from making appropriate decisions.

Rowe says, 'We can't live without denying. We have to shut things out ... (but) if we go on denying what is happening, then we start to get into difficulties because our experience accords less and less with reality' (p. 67). As we grow, so we learn to deny. Sometimes these processes go too far and people get to live in their own cloud-cuckoo land. It is our suggestion that we should learn to shift from automatically denying to actively rejecting inappropriate alternatives.

Sometimes people fail to cope with their fears and this causes them anxiety. Below we explore this further; including looking at some of the negative costs of this that might not have been expected.

Special topic – anxiety and cognitive restriction

We said in Chapter 4 (see Table 4.2) that one of the problems which can arise from an imbalance between the Constancies is anxiety. In particular, if fearlessness levels are too low in relation to other Constancies, this may prove personally harmful: anxiety can be seen as unchecked awareness. People receive information from internal and external sources and may interpret it in a threatening manner, especially if they have such personal predispositions (i.e. they are 'anxious' types). In the FIT person these tendencies would be controlled by the other Constancies and the information and feedback used in a positive manner to inform choices. In the unFIT the Constancies may get out of kilter and increase the risk of fear turning into anxiety. We know that many apparently healthy working people do have problems with anxiety from time to time and that others are constantly anxious but can successfully mask their anxieties. In any organization, as many as 10 percent will have 'clinically relevant' levels of anxiety – with a further 20 percent at marginal levels. Some people cannot manage to cope themselves and get referred treatment from medics, psychologists, psychiatrists or other professionals. Anxiety is a major problem.

In an attempt to bring together different strands of research in anxiety, Professor Michael Eysenck considered the different aspects of anxiety from the study of personality traits, emotions and clinical psychology. He provided a unified theory of anxiety in a book called *Anxiety and Cognition* published in 1997. It proposes that the roots of anxiety are cognitive or psychological, rather than physiological, for example. Anxiety is one of the so-called 'Big Five' personality traits (see

Chapter 8), sometimes called neuroticism or negative affectivity. Being a personality trait implies that anxiety is a common characteristic on which all people can be rated: some have naturally higher levels than others do. Such people show a tendency to selectively attend to information, and to interpret it as threatening, even if it is presented incidentally. This suggests that the Awareness Constancy is also involved (the role of attention in anxiety has been extensively studied). Anxious individuals are more likely to be affected by their perceived levels of physiological arousal which suggests they tend to psychologically amplify the threats in the situation. This tendency to put a negative gloss on physiological information has a stronger external counterpart: research suggests that anxious people tend to feel worse because they appraise or evaluate environmental or external situations in a more negative way.

Eysenck's 'four factor theory' of anxiety says that cognitive biases, or psychological factors, affect how information is perceived and interpreted from the environment, from one's own behaviours, from one's own physiology, and from other cognitions. For example, those with generalized anxiety or 'free-floating' anxiety will show cognitive biases for all four factors. People who have panic disorders (without agoraphobia) will have a particular cognitive bias in terms of their physiological system; people with a social phobia, a bias of the behavioural dimension; and those with a specific phobia (e.g. spiders), a bias in the environmental factor. Eysenck contrasts anxious people with what he calls 'repressors' who strategically avoid things that provide potential threats. Such individuals have the opposite cognitive biases of anxious people and are less likely to be influenced by them.

The fact that anxiety and its understanding is so dependent upon the influence of personal attributions, interpretations and cognitive biases reinforces the dynamic power of the individual which is central to FIT. In the context of this discussion too, it suggests that there will be potential benefits, as well as costs, to being potentially anxious. Such individuals may have a greater capacity for FITness because they are exercising the relevant psychological apparatus – what they need to do is to put this to good effect (FITness) instead of ill-effect (anxiety). According to FITness this requires a boosting of other relevant Constancies to harmonize them, rather than a reduction in the Fearlessness Constancy, which simply serves to decrease the person's potential.

Anxious people develop cognitive biases that restrict the way they perceive the world. We call this 'cognitive restriction' because these biases are almost always negative and result in the individual being less able to deal with the richness of information they receive from their environment. Anxious people are more likely to show:

- more mistakes and accidents;
- intolerance of ambiguity/uncertainty;
- reduction in cognitive and behavioural repertoires;
- less willingness to use new solutions;
- retreat to old habits/behaviours/solutions;
- a diminution in their receptiveness to change;
- greater negativity;
- enhanced feeling of vulnerability for new initiatives;
- lowered creativity;
- desire for the known 'comfort zone'.

For example, in one research sample of our own, the people at work who score more highly on anxiety made more everyday lapses of memory and slips of action which suggests they may be more accident prone. The same group of people were also asked to do an unusual categorization task to assess the effects of anxiety on more fundamental mental processes. When judging how 'typical' certain examples were of a particular category (e.g. a robin or a parakeet as birds), anxious people are much less likely to rate untypical examples as members of the category, even when they are. It seems that anxious people have a smaller range of tolerance for ambiguity and complexity. Other research has also shown that anxiety interferes with 'working memory' which is involved in the ongoing performance of some tasks, and that it seems to lead to less extensive or elaborate initial consideration of information before it is put into memory for processing further (called 'encoding').

Balance

We know instinctively what is meant by balance although we often lose it and very few can walk a tightrope (let alone at a height which also makes them frightened). Balancing the various aspects of our lives and ourselves is, we believe, essential for a sound self-identity, self-esteem, well-being and sustained development. Research evidence also strongly supports the view that balance is good for a positive home and work life: a person who is 'out of kilter' in one area is likely to 'infect' the other areas of their lives with the same problems. This is because the various areas of our lives are all interdependent on each other: the nature of our work, for example, affects how we spend our leisure-time and the quality of family life. It does this in some obvious ways: people who spend a lot of time at work, for example, are less likely to have good marriages and family lives simply because they are not present often enough. Those who change jobs regularly, whose jobs require them to move geographic locations a great deal, or who have jobs that entail spending long times away from home, are likely to suffer as a consequence of the family disruption entailed. There are, however, less obvious effects too. For example, the work one does also affects one's own health and the health and life expectancy of those around us, as Professor Fletcher has shown in his own empirical research on occupational mortality and the transmission of occupational stress between marital partners. The work we do 'spills over' into our social life, our leisure activities, and even influences our partners' disease risks. We cannot segmentalize the different areas of our lives, even if we consider them as separate. In an article in *Fortune* magazine in March 1997 Betsy Morris shows that having a family is bad for getting on in companies. One demonstration of this is what she calls the 'two-career penalty': well-qualified men whose wives did not work earned 32 percent more than equally qualified men whose wives did do paid employment. They were also more likely to be promoted to top management.

There are many other examples of spillover. Having an active job, for example, makes it more likely that an individual will have active leisure-time pursuits and be generally more active in the community. A sedentary job makes an inactive life outside work more likely. It also seems that leisure and work factors both contribute to well-being and health. It has been firmly established by Professor David Fryer from the United Kingdom that unemployment is bad for personal health as well as being associated with greater levels of family abuse. More recent research by Professor Seppo Iso-Ahola from the University of Maryland, USA, also suggests that a positive seeking out, or active pursuance, of leisure-time activities is more beneficial for mental and physical health than escapist leisure activities. Active leisure (which may promote positive 'flow' experiences *á la* Professor Csikszentmihalyi, discussed on pages 152–3), also seems to provide a buffer against the stressful effects of demanding jobs, possibly because they promote a greater feeling of personal control in people.

One consequence of lack of balance between work and home life is an increase in what is known as 'work–family conflict' which arises from having to manage the demands of the work role and the family role. The conflict arises because participation in one of the roles makes participation in the other more difficult. This in turn will result in lower work and life satisfaction. Balancing these conflicts is essential because, almost by definition, such conflicts will always exist. Research has shown that work–family conflict is associated with adverse health and well-being. For example, Professor Michael Frone from the Research Institute on Addiction, New York, and colleagues published a study of this in the UK *Journal of Occupational and Organizational Psychology* (1997, 70: 325–335). In a four-year study of 267 employed parents, they found that the effects of family matters interfering with work included elevated depression, hypertension and poor physical health. When work interfered with family roles there was a marked increase in alcohol consumption.

In general, achieving balance requires becoming the architect of one's own conflict profile (i.e. deciding which conflicts to accept) because zero conflict is not usually possible. We suggest that the FIT person is more likely to see the need for taking personal charge of the conflicts and to achieve the balance which works for their situation: they are more likely to come to an appropriate set of arrangements.

Research also shows that balance is one of the most important contributors in achieving high levels of personal effectiveness and performance in one's work. It is counterproductive to work too hard, just as it is bad not to work hard enough. The balance principle says that efficiency and effectiveness in any area of life is compromised by over-focus in any other area.

The mastery–intimacy balance

Balance is not just a matter of getting work and non-work in perspective. The balance needs to be wider than that. Joan Kofodimos, in her book *Balancing Act* published in 1993, suggests that managers and executives are often too focused on the drive for mastery in both their work and home lives: they become 'mastery-oriented' as a means of clarifying their own identity, enhancing their self-esteem and feeling fulfilled. This mastery-orientation emphasizes logic, people's task performance, expects high standards for self and others, is built on a desire to be in charge, needs aggression and confidence to be sustained, and puts an emphais on activity and productivity. Kofodimos goes on to show how a mastery-oriented approach causes problems for many people and their organizations, including an inherent reluctance to change, stress, poor performance, an unhelpful power focus and the constant need to be right.

Kofodimis argues that it is necessary to balance the mastery-approach with what she calls the 'intimacy-oriented approach'. She says that people get their lives out of balance because they avoid intimacy in their work and home lives. The intimacy-oriented approach is character-ized by an emphasis on one's own and others' feelings, a concern with what people need and want, a tolerance of weaknesses, the need to co-operate and connect with others, and to express emotions and be playful in life and work. Unfortunately, Kofodimis says, people become used to a mastery–intimacy imbalance which they perpetuate by focusing their energies on work and striving for mastery in all they engage in. This also makes their personal lives seem mundane and makes relaxation very difficult. The mastery-orientation also means people take on competitive leisure activities, structured vacations, suffer constant impatience and frustration, feel rushed and often pressured by deadlines, and try to control and manage everything. As a consequence they have distanced personal relationships, few personal friends and are reluctant to ask others for help.

To achieve mastery–intimacy balance requires the individual to take a good look at their own internal drivers, to assess what their current approach and aspirations are, and to develop a vision for life priorities. The individual also needs an action plan consistent with it, which ensures that both mastery and intimacy approaches are given due opportunity to flourish.

The self and balance

The emphasis that Joan Kofodimis places on giving intimacy a chance is akin to putting yourself more in the balance picture. Perhaps the most difficult aspect of balance is to give sufficient prominence to oneself and one's own growth and development. This is an area that has not been researched a great deal. There has been some research looking at such matters as the effects of mismatch between people's skills and the demands of their job (poor fit causing problems), or the inner conflicts that may arise when personal values have to be compromised by outside demands at work or socially. In general, the need to give sufficient focus to the inner self, and to balance this with outer work and non-work aspects, is something that individuals give little notice to because they generally concentrate only on external matters. We suggest, however, that the self should have a greater prominence otherwise real balance will not be achieved. We suggest that balancing internal drivers with the demands of the external environment is essential for proper self-identity, self-respect, well-being and to sustain any personal development.

Balance requires one to be in harmony with oneself and all other important dimensions of life. We suggest that without self-harmony, people can never achieve harmony with others or, therefore, the other aspects of their lives. Balance is a determinant of the respect and responsibility that we have for ourselves and others; emotional autonomy; flexibility; realism; and our ability to focus on one dimension of our lives while at the same time having the ability to de-focus as and when appropriate. This focus on the self in the balance equation implies the necessity of:

- Seeing yourself as the centre of your own universe. This will enable you to see others in the same light. It provides justification for the development of moral values. It helps in developing a strong sense of self-responsibility and raising the demands and expectations of oneself.

- The ability to develop a good relationship with yourself. There is a need for proactive self-reflection to develop a realistic and objective self-appraisal system. A reactive system is also necessary because things do not always go as expected.

- Eliminating any overwhelming focus on external needs. External needs are potentially of negative value and are more likely to lead to distress than joy. Needs met by external factors are short lived and rely on constant reassurance. In the same light, needs or expectations forced upon us by external forces are, we suggest, more likely to be unhealthy partly because we have little control over the external forces. External needs are often a legacy of our history and have little productive value: they are often destructive.

- Developing the ability to focus and de-focus as and when is appropriate. Lack of balance occurs when we become over-focused on a particular dimension (e.g. work, leisure, self). From a young age we are encouraged to apply ourselves in a highly focused fashion. Single-mindedness is lauded as a positive attribute. This can be counterproductive. FITness suggests the need to develop from single-mindedness to multi-mindedness. A single-minded focus is likely to be related to inflexibility and insecurity. Balance allows us to focus on the task at hand but be aware of all other relevant factors, both internal and external. An over-focused or single-minded approach increases the likelihood of missing important information relevant to the current situation. Our attention gets kidnapped by the over-focus and creates a sort of tunnel vision.

Balancing self, balancing elements

In order to be well-balanced two things are necessary:

- That the 'self' be at the centre.

- That the other important life elements are in harmony with each other and with the self.

Figure 7.1 represents the aspects of self and outside elements that need balancing. The analogy with a wheel is useful. At the centre of the wheel, the hub, is the self.

We suggest that the individual needs to perceive themselves at the centre of the balance wheel in order to be able to achieve a balance of the spoke elements. This is because it is they who have to effect any changes in the external elements of their life.

The spokes of the wheel represent the external elements. These will vary in the specifics from person to person, although the generic categories relating to work and leisure will be present for most. Some individuals may have their own elements (spokes), and others may not have some (e.g. no partner, or children).

Each element or spoke contains three parts that are indicators of:

- Value, i.e. the importance the person attributes to that element.

- Satisfaction, i.e. how happy or satisfied the person is with that element.

- Focus, i.e. the degree of focus or effort put into that element.

Each of these aspects is important in the balance equation. For example, a person may be happily married, consider their partner very important/valuable to them, but not focus on them much of the time. This may produce problems because of the lack of balance within this element. The 'self' should also be evaluated according to the same three measures which shows how much a person perceives their own worth, as well as the degree to which they are 'centred'. For example, if they score low on any of the three self-measures, they cannot be said to be properly centred.

Balance allows one to see the dimensions of one's life in an objective manner, including oneself. Balance is treating each dimension of our lives

FIGURE 7.1   The wheel of balance

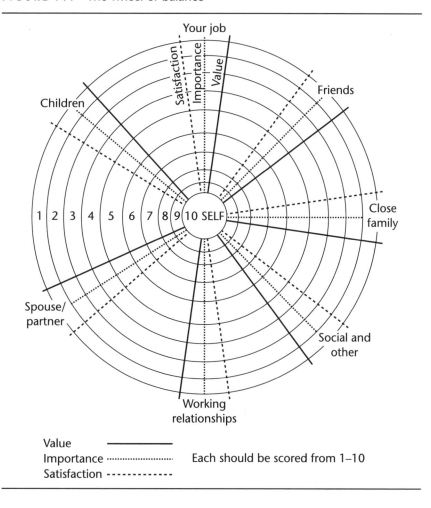

Value ————————

Importance ·······························

Satisfaction - - - - - - - - - - -

Each should be scored from 1–10

with equal respect and responsibility. Balance is ensuring that the various dimensions or elements do not compete with each other and that no one dimension is more important than another.

Achieving balance between the various aspects of one's life is not easy for several reasons:

■   Over-focusing in any area causes imbalance.

■   People see themselves as being constrained by situations when they are not. They see, for example, the need to work many hours, or they have financial commitments which are problematic for them.

Such aspects may be due to lack of balance or focus, taking account of the person's situation and options.

- In some areas people do not have sufficient freedom to achieve adequate balance, and may rightly feel unable to take alternative courses of action. It is well known that lack of discretion or autonomy in the workplace, for example, is one of the most stressful aspects of work – it is not the demands of work, but largely the constraints of work that harm people. Many companies do not empower their employees sufficiently. Such constraints operate in other areas of life too. It is common, for example, for partners to constrain each other out of fear, jealousy, laziness and other negative emotions.

- Knowing what constitutes balance requires a detached look at one's life. Many cannot do this without help. A major problem in achieving balance is being able to detach one's involvement with one dimension while we deal effectively with another. Failure to do this causes us to make biased and inappropriate decisions: one dimension contaminates the other and causes imbalance.

Special topic – workaholism

Some people work too much. Employed people now work the equivalent of an extra month per year (i.e. 120 hours) than they did 50 years ago. About 50 percent of executives work over 10 hours a day and most take work home at night and weekends. The position is even worse for entrepreneurs and those trying to grow their businesses. More and more people base their lives and the reasons for their existence on their work. Without it they have no self-identity and no internal purpose. They are victims of Parkinson's Law which says that work expands to fit the time available to do it in. They expand work by devoting more time to it and most believe they work effectively throughout. The term 'workaholic' has been coined to describe such people. Oates in his book *Confessions of a Workaholic* published in 1971 was one of the first to use the term and attempt to define it. He defines a workaholic as a person whose need for work has become compulsive. It is so excessive that it creates noticeable disturbance or interference with his/her bodily health, personal happiness, interpersonal relations and social functioning.

The workaholic is out of balance, is inefficient, infects others with inefficiency. They are more likely to be stressed, to become ill, to make others ill, to breed antagonism and destroy the most valuable asset a company has: the human resource. It is perverse that workaholics are often seen as champions of profit and the core of a good successful company. Professor Fletcher has suggested what he calls *Fletcher's Law* which encapsulates the problems:

> For every hour *worked* over 7 in a day, efficiency is compromised by 5 minutes for every hour worked. The longer this persists, the greater the costs in efficiency.
>
> Corollary 1: People do not see this, and organizations do not believe it.
>
> Corollary 2: For every apparent gain in work performance, there is an equal or greater negative organizational cost.

Not all workaholics are the same or have the same motivations. Oates, for example, outlined a number of different types:

(i)   *The Classic Workaholic* who is over-committed to the job and the organization, tends to be a perfectionist who shows intolerance of incompetence and lack of commitment in others. Such people need to refocus their priorities to achieve a better balance.

(ii) *The Situational Workaholic* who is only workaholic because of some felt necessity due to circumstances, such as being new to the job, being low down in the pecking order, or having to work hard out of economic necessity. Such people appear to have better balanced priorities, but are victims of circumstance. They need to change the circumstances.

(iii) *The Pseudo-Workaholic* who does it for show. They look like the classic cases but are workaholic out of fear of creating the wrong impression, or because they are power hungry and want to 'get on'. These people need to concentrate on making sure they are happy with their motivations and to ensure their choices are not fear-led.

(iv) *The Escapist Posing as a Workaholic* has personal problems and uses work as a shield to hide behind. These people need to learn that this is a different trap, not an escape route. They need to tackle the real issues.

Overwork is bad because, as well as compromising FITness and health, it affects:

- *Your physiology:* Overwork causes elevations of stress hormones and disruption of healthy bodily functioning. People ignore the warning signs: colds linger, health problems get worse, they become irritable, get somatic complaints, indigestion, insomnia, increased alcohol intake, drinking more coffee to keep going, and not having the time to say good morning.

■ *Your decision making and vision:* The longer people work and the more out of balance they are the less inventive they become, the more they use old habits as solutions to problems, and the narrower their visions and goals. They are also more likely to make errors of judgement and to show tunnel vision.

■ *Your work performance:* Many studies have shown that the principles behind Fletcher's Law hold for manual and managerial jobs. Excessive work not only reduces the rate of output per hour, but also is accompanied by an increase in absences for sickness and accidents. Many individuals, when faced with excessive working hours, will pace themselves (usually unconsciously) to keep going and will periodically go sick to recuperate from cumulative states of fatigue.

■ *Your health:* At least 5 percent of GNP (Gross National Product) is lost every year due to sickness, poor productivity, staff turnover, and premature retirement as a result of the stress of work. Research shows that those who overwork suffer more health problems. Those with an over-focus on work are more likely to suffer 'burnout' which is 'a process in which individuals become exhausted by making excessive demands on energy strength'.

■ *Your spouse, friends and colleagues:* The workaholic is a stress carrier who can easily infect others with workaholism, as well as increasing aggression and hostility. Charles Garfield in his book *Peak Performers: The New Heroes in American Business* emphasizes the effects on work culture: 'People get drawn into workaholism. If senior managers believe that work addiction is the best thing – come in early, stay late – there is tremendous pull for other people to adopt addict styles of work.' Workaholism practised by just one member of a working group can suck the spirit out of a team, and a workaholic placed in a lead or management position is one of the most divisive forces roaming the corridors of the industrialized world. There are obvious consequences for home life and relationships with family members, such as marital problems, lack of quality time with spouse and children and leisure time spent alone. There is also evidence from Professor Fletcher's work on the transmission of occupational stress between marital partners that occupational stress resulting from workaholism affects the life expectancy and cause of death of the incumbent and that these work stressors may be transmitted through psychological mechanism to the worker's *spouse*. Spouses have similar mortality risks and causes of death that can be attributed to the husband's job, although it has recently been shown that women in high-status jobs do transmit to husbands if they are in lower-status jobs. Therefore the psychological effects of overwork should not be expected to be confined only to the individuals themselves who overwork.

Self-responsibility

Self-responsibility is necessary for self-freedom, but, like freedom, comes with obligations and requires constant maintenance. If we allow others to determine the broad and finer shape of our lives we do not have these obligations, but by abandoning control and self-autonomy we also forgo freedom, choice and any reason for complaints. Self-responsibility is the key to growth and development, but is also a difficult concept because many people do not see the degree to which they can be responsible for what happens to them and how they unconsciously shape their world. It is our contention that taking responsibility can change almost anything that influences us. FITness does not believe that the ubiquitous 'they' are responsible for anything of great causal significance. If you want to be self-responsible, always assume that everything past, present or future which involves you directly or indirectly is down to you.

A well-researched concept which has relevance for the issue of self-responsibility is Professor John Rotter's seminal work on the *'locus of control' (or LOC)* published in *Psychological Monographs* in 1966. According to LOC, individuals can be described by the degree to which they see themselves in control of external events. Those people who have high beliefs about their abilities to control events are described as having an *'internal LOC'*, whereas those with low expectancies – the people who see outside factors as controlling what happens – are said to have an *'external LOC'*. There has been a considerable amount of research on the concept of LOC. Individuals with an internal LOC, compared to external, are likely to be more motivated; to do better at work; to be less prone to impatience and irritability; to be more satisfied; keener to achieve; to report higher levels of autonomy and discretion in what they do; to adopt more of a transformational (visionary and inspirational), as opposed to a transactional (contingent-reward based), style of leadership; and even to have the ability to consciously direct the events of their lucid dreams.

The essence of internal LOC is that such individuals are less dependent in their perceptions and actions on external factors: they drive things to a greater extent than individuals with an external LOC focus. This is central to the Self-responsibility Constancy. Another similar concept is that of *'field-dependence/independence'* which relates more to how people perceive their environment. The person with high self-responsibility, high internal LOC will also be *field independent.* This means that they are less dependent upon external cues, and less affected by them, in their perceptual and other judgements. Field-independent people even see things differently inasmuch as they are not influenced as much by cues which might be misleading (as in illusions, for example). They are also more reliant on the objective information provided, whereas the field-dependent person is more likely to conform in their judgements, to acquiesce and to be more reliant on others for self-assessment.

Special topic – emotional intelligence

Emotional life has its ups and downs. It is a key aspect of human life and doubtless leads people to make wrong choices as well as right ones, in spite of what reason would have us do. Emotions interfere with many cognitive processes by reducing the capacity of our 'working memory' stores which are central to nearly all ongoing tasks and situations, they influence logical reasoning, and upset our attentional control by distracting attention. Emotions can, therefore, have a whole range of negative consequences in the way they narrow the options and constrain the appreciation of useful information: they create 'tunnel vision' in decision making. The powerful effect emotion exerts on our reasoning and everyday decisions, including the way we behave, has led some commentators to the view that a person's ability to control their emotions can matter more than their IQ. Daniel Goleman (1995), for example, provides many cases of intelligent people doing stupid and illogical things because they did not control their emotions and feelings. Goleman popularized the phrase 'emotional intelligence' to refer to the ability to know and manage one's own emotions as well as reading and dealing with them in other people. He suggests – and evidence would support him – that people who develop these emotional skills will be more balanced and effective in all spheres of their lives. Emotional intelligence involves such factors as self-awareness, showing empathy and social deftness, motivating oneself, persisting despite difficulties, being able to control one's impulses and to delay gratification and reward, regulating one's moods and ensuring they do not interfere with one's decisions. People who develop emotional intelligence will have the benefits of being more at peace with themselves, more successful at what they do, and have better intimate relationships and friends. Those who fail to develop emotional intelligence will be more at risk of having poor relationships, becoming clinically depressed and anxious, bad health and generally a less successful and fulfilling life.

Emotional intelligence, or as we prefer to call it 'emotional autonomy', necessarily requires an internal self-monitoring, and the ability to perceive the emotions as they are happening and to learn the situations with which the various emotions are associated. In relation to FIT theory this would be captured by the awareness process – being awake to the various kinds of influences and feedback, including emotions, which arise constantly. What FIT does in addition, however, is to provide an internal metric for personal measurement (i.e. the other four Constancies). How FIT a person is will be a good predictor of the degree to which they can use their emotions in an intelligent manner. But FITness also predicts how they use other kinds of feedback in decision making too. People get feedback from all sorts of processes that they either do not perceive, or ignore, including from their emotions. The FIT individual, or one in training, will endeavour to become aware and act on the basis of all these sources – not just emotions. In FIT theory, emotional intelligence is but one of the important by-products of acting with Integrity. Trying to focus on just the area of emotional control would not in itself lead to the same wide-ranging benefits of being FIT. It is somewhat akin to concentrating on one's heart rate or blood pressure in physical fitness – important, perhaps, but not the key to fitness and health. Emotional autonomy comes from being FIT and is not, in itself, the main goal. FITness also shifts the focus from emotional autonomy as being good for the individual (because they will do better in their lives) towards being generally beneficial.

FIT people are emotional and have extreme emotions but are not seduced by the emotions in an historical way, i.e. they don't become chronically depressed because that requires a history.

Morality and Ethics

The Morality and Ethics Constancy has a different kind of status to the other Constancies because it concentrates on ensuring that decisions and actions satisfy a social, as opposed to individual dimension. Being moral and ethical in our sense, however, requires that the boundaries of acceptable behaviour and decisions are very much individual in the sense that they are core aspects of the person: they happen to have a social context that defines them. The FIT person operates with a strong moral and ethical code which they own and accept 100 percent. Morality and ethics do, however, have many guises and levels from the spiritual, religious, human rights, through to legal frameworks for moral and ethical maintenance. But these aspects, however relevant to the FIT person, do not dictate their moral and ethical code – that is defined by the person themselves taking account of relevant factors and the other four Constancies.

Special topic – business ethics: 'short-termism' and long-term success

Business ethics has taken on a sharper profile in recent years owing to such factors as the increasing globalization of business; the greater interrelationships between all parts of the business and money markets; the increasing influence of some companies (e.g. media) in everyday life; the development of information technology as a storage and selling device, and the greater chance for 'insider' information to distort markets, rewards and returns; the increasing demands on worker's greater efficiency; calls for greater transparency in the market; and the disparities between different labour markets and their potential exploitation by global businesses. An immoral or unethical act can have major impact in today's media-enveloped world because of its wider potential conse-quences for others and the greater number of people who learn about it. Business ethics is big business.

An important basis of all human transactions is trust. This is particularly key in business transactions where business success depends on the buyer having trust in the seller (however misplaced this may be in the longer term). Selling in a business context, in the widest meaning of the word, is often based on the degree to which a person has been successful in selling themselves in the interaction or exchange. Therefore, a major issue in business is perceived moral integrity. The FIT notion of Integrity is somewhat different from moral integrity, although it does encompass it. It would be our contention that just as FIT Integrity is a quality that 'shines' through and is perceived by others (sometimes jealously), the same is true of moral integrity. We also believe that moral integrity pays off in the longer term for the individual, even if there are sometimes short-term costs. Failure to achieve a target in one month due to keeping one's moral integrity intact is rewarded with better figures subsequently. In a review paper on business ethics published in the journal *A European Review* in 1998 (7(2): 111–124), Professor Johan Verstraeten from the University of Leuven in the Netherlands concluded that ethical behaviour makes good business sense as well as being more rational than acting unethically. He quotes a number of examples, including the fact that the 15 Fortune 500 companies that adhered to an ethical code had over double the profits growth of those that did not have such a code. Ethical issues have also been shown to have a dramatic effect on stock market valuation. More practical aspects of business ethics – those that are related to such things as customer relations, product safety and labour relations – are also related to better long-term company results.

Professor Verstraeten outlines some of the problems for companies that do not act in a moral and ethical way. He also believes that the moral and ethical guidelines must come from a positive set of organizational ethical values that have a strong foundation in the social and religious context of the society in which it operates. For Verstraeten, acting and deciding without a normative foundation of ethics and morals is a dangerous illusion. He rightly says that most managers operate on the basis of ethics which might be termed 'economicism': the market goal will in the end benefit the society because it has in-built corrective mechanisms. A smaller number act 'morally' out of 'conventionalism': they simply act according to the recognized values of the society. We agree that neither of these is adequate: morality and ethics based on either competitiveness or economic incentives are vacuous. We also agree that companies that do not act ethically and morally will lose their legitimacy. However, we do not believe a normative moral code should be the foundation on which to build a business ethic for an individual or an organization. That foundation must be based on the understanding or ideal that FIT individuals do take account of moral and ethical matters, that such people will impact on organizations and business life, and that the individual, not the society or some aggregate of it (like an organization), holds the moral and ethical balance.

Essentially our view is saying that any decision or action that is not based on an individual's FIT perspective cannot be justified by recourse to 'rules' of society. There will always be misfit and moral tension in such a state and there will always be immorality and non-ethical behaviour. In FIT the individual has the power to act morally and ethically and will exercise that freedom. Differences between people will be a matter of analysis and decision, not of edict and rules which are blind to other

FIT-related matters. In the end, acting morally and with Integrity requires a moral identity that has to be individually centred if it is to have an individual force and justification.

The position of morals and ethics in FIT is, therefore, definitely not one of moral absolutism. We offer no list of moral rules to which the FIT or unFIT should adhere. It is our view that absolute moral rules are themselves immoral precisely because they do not permit of adequate consideration of contextual matters: this is something that cannot be done properly in advance of the situation, or without proper considera-tion of all the circumstances at the time. Moreover, it is often simply not possible to identify all the relevant 'stakeholders' in an issue before the actual situation arises.

The position we adopt, therefore, could be considered a kind of what is called 'ethical relativism'. It is not, however, one that permits individuals freedom to do what they want – a charge often levied rightly at many relative stances. Unlike many other relative moral and ethical positions, FIT morals do not stand alone: decisions and actions are guided by the five Constancies, not just by one. In FIT no decision is purely one-dimensional – ethical or not, moral or not – because the decision or action is judged by whether it is FIT or not. That requires a consideration of all five Constancies. FITness replaces the moral and ethical absolutes with the need to make FIT decisions. In this sense it could be called a 'consequentialist' position, where the individual acts of FITness combine to make for an inherently ethical and moral society, but not one with prescriptive lists of what is and is not morally and ethically permissible. It is utilitarian for both the individual and the society and espouses a view that takes neither a long nor short-term perspective, but a reasonable one. FITness has in-built practical morality informed by all relevant aspects. FITness is an individual matter but one that does not permit of hedonistic self-interest, only FIT self-interest, which considers aspects from all points of view. In a sense the FIT position neutralizes the need for moral and ethical debates in isolation of other aspects (in FIT these other aspects are covered by Balance, Self-responsibility, Awareness and Fearlessness). FITness is the 'categorical imperative' (to steal a phrase from the 18th-century philosopher, Immanuel Kant). It is an imperative with a self-regulatory and self-regulating framework. Another way of putting it – in terms relevant to the debate about business ethics – is to say that the social responsibility of the individual is to increase their FITness.

CHAPTER EIGHT

(Inner) FITness in context

Most of the practical work and research of psychologists is backward-looking in the sense that it is searching for the causes of, and influences on, human behaviour in all its guises. It generally advances by deconstruction, simplification and then the gradual enlargement of models based on empirical falsification and experimentation. Theories are constructed which demonstrate how previous experiences change the way in which people behave. These past behaviours and events are used to predict future consequences, in the same way that economic models forecast markets and economic changes. The psychological histories might take account of influences over just a few milliseconds – the blink of an eye. For example, in some perceptual experiments it has been shown that things people say they have not seen (but which were presented to them for a short time) influence them. Other research has proved that people cannot see things which are shown to influence their decision making (some of these effects are given labels such as 'backward masking', 'priming', 'subliminal perception' and 'blindsight' and have proved invaluable in the understanding of the brain and its cognitive processes). Alternatively, the psychological histories are presumed to wreak their effects over many years as, for example, with chronic stress, and many psychotherapeutic interpretations of adult dysfunction. Perhaps the Freudian approaches are amongst the best known of this kind, but there are a plethora of others covering all sorts of influences from subtle cognitive processing to the structure of social behaviour.

The psychological models constructed to explain decisions and behaviour are gradually refined with new evidence of previously omitted influences, newly found synergies and interactions amongst factors. The factors that shape behaviour and learning are used to develop theories of perception, learning, motivation, personality, social aspects and illness. This is how most psychological science develops. The backward-looking methods and techniques have served the discipline well. Many major advances in our understanding of people and society have been made. Theories of how we learn, for example, have been very important in shaping many aspects of modern society, from the design of machines and buildings, consumer behaviour and advertising strategy, to such aspects as doctor–patient interaction, the way interviews should be conducted and company training best done.

One aspect of this approach or emphasis is that, by definition and theoretical necessity, people, and their component processes, are seen as captured by an analysis of their past history – however short-term the time over which that is considered. It is this history that gives them their identity and their problems. That is one legacy of Freud. He was the father of this historical analysis that dominates psychology.

The approach taken in *(Inner) FITness*™ theory is different. Instead of explaining the past, it looks forwards and is a theory that is based on the potential of people, not on their constraints. It does not deconstruct the past, but presents the building blocks for a personal future. It is not Panglossian; it is a different and no less rigorous or scientific perspective. But it does require a different kind of consideration of many key issues, many of which are seen as non-questions from this future-looking perspective.

This is a position that is part of a new approach to science and investigation, which has been suggested by Professor Fletcher. He calls this 'SCIchange' to signify that its emphasis is on the analysis of circumstances that are most conducive to improving or changing a state of affairs. SCIchange presents a very different set of criteria for doing science and evaluating it. The methodological approach of SCIchange is also different from the traditional scientific methods. In the traditional science the emphasis is on understanding the theoretical mechanisms which underlie a phenomenon or explain an aspect of the world. Models, tests and an emphasis on falsification and refinement do this where such issues as methodology, experimental design, robustness, detachment, simulation and control are the watchwords and determinants of quality. SCIchange does not emphasize such aspects – they are secondary to the change and influence that occur in any situation. The emphasis is on bringing about the situations that will effect most change in the object of the study (this might be in terms of health, scores on a psychological or medical test, changes in performance, reductions in negative things such as stress, crime, smoking, or whatever). In the FIT context it is improved well-being and performance. The SCIchange approach need not be any less 'scientific', although the criteria for the science will be different from normal.

Table 8.1 shows some of the contrasts between the traditional approaches to science and the SCIchange framework.

SCIchange is not an appropriate framework for all scientific studies because for some areas of 'pure' science it is necessary to learn about the actual mechanisms underlying the object of investigation. This is an

TABLE 8.1 The contrasts between the traditional scientific methods and SCIchange

SCIchange	*Traditional science*
Criteria of success:	
Degree of change	Stability
Effects observed	Understanding mechanisms
Innovation	Control
Pragmatism	Theory refinement
Benefit	Robustness of theory
Presence of effect	Conditions precisely defined
Enhancing change	Enhancing theory
Success at effecting change	A 'winning' single theory
Aspects that characterize the approach:	
Circumstances for change	Theoretical factors
Multi-dimensional	Single factors
Ambiguity	Clarity
Doubt about 'causes'	Certainty
Openness	Entrenchment and defence
Multi-method/approach	Single method/approach
Complication	Deconstruction/simplification
Experiment and hunch	Experiment and step-by-step
Assumption of multiple factors involved	Factors can be isolated separately
Constellational view	Casual view
Do	Observe
Involvement	Detachment
Reality	Laboratory
Reality frameworks	Analogy, theory and models
Gradual simplification	Gradual elaboration
Focus on dependent variable (i.e. the benefit)	Focus on independent variables (i.e. the conditions)
Soft expansive science	Narrow methods/hard science

essential aspect of some branches of medicine and biology, for example: it is essential to be sure of the precise biological or neurological action of drugs and medicine. However, for many scientific investigations a SCIchange, as opposed to a traditional scientific approach, would be more useful, even though die-hards would maintain the need for a traditional approach. In many of these cases the science masquerades as 'practically mechanistic' when the models that underlie it are not models of reality, but models of abstraction in the same way that billiard balls were once a useful way of representing atoms. Most science, even in the natural and human sciences, advances by the refinement of analogy and abstract theory, and not by describing the actual mechanisms, or the abstract but isomorphic bases.

A grand theory

The FIT framework is something of a 'grand theory' that involves many different facets of the psychology of people. Most theories do not set out to establish such a broad relevance and are not, therefore, open to discussion from all these fronts. The perspective developed here was originally an attempt to explain why some people suffer from occupational stress and others do not appear to. The theory also had to explain why it appeared that occupational stressors were transmitted to others not exposed directly to the dangers in the workplace in such a way as to influence their causes of death.

A common way of increasing the predictability of a theory is to add factors or variables to it, for example to gradually extend the number or range of variables (e.g. from single work factors, through individual variables, domestic, social and environmental factors). As the ideas developed it became clear that a broader and simpler framework was necessary. Instead of adding complexity the interpretation was reduced to one dimension – what was then called the 'cognitive architecture' of the individuals. It was proposed that the work a person does subtly influences the way they think and behave – their cognitive architecture – and that this determined disease risk, life expectancy and cause of death to an important extent. Since a primary mediator of the outcomes (strain, disease, anxiety, poor sleep, diet, low satisfaction, etc.) was hypothesized to be a psychological mechanism, the transmission of stress risks to others became easily explicable. The hypothesized 'cognitive architecture' was passive inasmuch as it was presumed to have influence through unconscious or unheeded processes and had outcomes that were hidden or non-apparent or which took many years to have an influence (such as diseases). In the area of occupational stress it is usually true that most people are not aware of their level of strain, and are certainly not able to get an accurate account of the factors that determine it (even though they think they can). In this sense the methods of psychology are bound to fail to provide an understanding of the issues they attempt to, because they often rely on tapping these 'unconscious' processes by direct questioning of the individuals.

It is clear that passive mechanisms can only account for a small proportion of the factors that influence outcomes, and that there are many outcomes to which they may not be relevant. For example, even though unconscious or subconscious processes clearly influence many of the things we humans do it seems equally obvious that we actively and consciously alter our decisions and behaviours, albeit often poorly. The FIT conceptual framework attempts to add this active or conscious dimension. It is suprising how much of psychological theory, relevant to all manner of issues, pays scant attention to the role of active, conscious, effortful, person-centred decisions or attempts to alter 'natural' outcomes. FIT puts the person firmly at the centre. Indeed FIT suggests that the person needs to be more firmly centred as the causal influencer of decisions and behaviours that have previously been seen as the province of personal history and outer circumstances. People need to be more firmly in control of themselves. Even if they cannot control their environments in the workplace or at home, and even if they can exercise only minor influence on how others behave, they should attempt at least some control over themselves. In many ways it is a paradoxical aspect of human behaviour that most people attempt to control the factors outside their immediate sphere of influence (i.e. others, or aspects of the environment) and pay little real attention to controlling or influencing themselves. They get stressed and find life difficult as a result. This is not suprising. FIT tries to redress this imbalance.

Figure 2.1 illustrates this 'responsibility bias'. Essentially it shows that the individual (the 'I' or Integrity) is under constant pressure to allow outside influences to engulf them. These pressures would include all prior learning, genes, social pressures and mores, their personality, needs and other factors. The arrows pointing outwards show the pressure. These are meant to depict the centrifugal forces operating to dilute the self-identity and felt self-responsibility of the individual. It is hypothesized that although the person needs to be sensitive to the outside influences, and to respond accordingly, there is an appropriate point at which to draw the circle around the person, so as not to allow the outside influences to become negative (called here the 'Killing Fields'). Those who do not do this will become stressed, lose their identity in important ways, and show a general 'disintegration', including ill-health and lack of real success and high performance. Most people, it is suggested, build inflexible barriers at an inappropriate distance from the ideal. The FIT person learns from their past experiences, takes the positive from these outside influences, can demonstrate appropriate behavioural flexibility and response to these outside factors but retains a solid Identity core of self-identity and self-responsibility. Effectively, most people become prisoners of their history (by building rigid and solid walls), but the FIT use their past to good effect (by expanding their behavioural repertoire with experience). It is true that some people are dysfunctional because they are unable to be outward-looking to a sufficient degree: they are too insular and inflexible. A solid or frozen centre of the 'Integral Person' could represent these.

An individual has to chart a course through their life and environment. In the main people need to be influenced by their environment and experiences, but not become imprisoned or permanently biased by it – they need to retain their own measure of Integrity in order to gain optimally from the world and learn from it. Those who are able to learn this yet retain a psychological and behavioural flexibility, will be FIT. Those who are influenced by it, but do this without personal Integrity, will flounder in the longer term, even if their behavioural rigidity is an apparently successful outward recipe in the short term (see the different levels of Integrity in Figure 4.3).

The concept of FITness has put a number of other issues in a different perspective. Some of these are discussed below.

Self-regulation

Central to the notion of FITness is that people can regulate their own behaviour and decisions, and that they do so according to some internal standards or goals. In FIT theory we suggest that the personal standard which could usefully guide behaviour and decision making is what we call Integrity and its dependants, the Constancies. Is this a reasonable assumption?

There is an increasing volume of evidence showing that 'cognitions' or thoughts can and do guide behaviour, and that the FIT theory is a practical reality. It is now understood that people filter the information they receive from the world through 'schemas' or 'bias filters' that are an integral part of the memory systems central to all decisions and actions. These schemas guide our behaviour in important ways and can themselves be affected by unconscious as well as purposive factors. The FIT Constancies operationalize what we need to do in order to act with FIT Integrity. It would, however, be necessary to instil the Constancies as part of our cognitive architecture, or automatic hard-wired processes, in order to be able to act in a consistently FIT way. There are two reasons to suggest that this is possible:

■ We can make behaviours more likely to occur by deciding to do so. We can learn to *consciously* bias our decisions and behaviour by considering a wider and wider range of what we do in terms of the Constancies. Consider the act of eating, for example, and the different levels at which we can consider this. We can be aware of the taste, texture and enjoyment of the act; the decision about what to eat and when; to considering dietary factors in our lifestyle; to even the social and environmental consequences of the eating.

■ Research shows that consciously biased schemas influence other actions that are controlled by related schemas because they too are activated by the actions. There is a spread of neural activation from one idea or action to related ones. For example, if you do an apparently innocuous task, which requires you to make sentences of some words given to you, the chances are that the type of words you have to unscramble will affect what you subsequently do. If the words happen to be associated with positive feelings towards others, you will be more likely to act positively in due course. If, however, the words were hostile in meaning, you will be more likely to act in a more hostile way despite the fact that the word task and the subsequent behaviour should not be connected. We connect them psychologically.

Human decisions and behaviours are always organized around goals, even when these are not explicit. FIT simply tries to make some of the goals more explicit, or to provide goals and standards against which to consider action and decisions. In general, people do organize their lives around implicit or explicit goals, both in the long and short term. Psychologists variously call these goals 'life tasks', 'personal strivings', 'current concerns' and 'personal projects'. Having such goals increases the meaningfulness we experience in living, as well as improving the chance of doing well. Interestingly, research has shown that hard goals (which are accepted) are associated with much higher levels of attainment than easily achievable goals, or simply leaving a person to 'do their best'. This is because goals or standards, such as always acting with Integrity in FITness:

- provide a focus for the individual

- produce more effort

- provide a strategic thrust

- provoke greater persistence and

- encourage a higher level of concentration.

FIT necessitates that individuals are self-regulating inasmuch as they can behave and decide with an internal standard in mind; that they are aware of the internal and external consequences of what they do and decide; and that they can learn to modify what they do as a result of experience. This requires that people can be self-regulating with respect to what they do. This requires the presence of feedback (necessary for learning and changing), the awareness of it, and the inclination to act on the basis of the feedback.

Cognitive Self-Regulation Theory, championed by Professors Charles Carver and Michael Schier of Miami and Carnegie Mellon Universities, provides a framework for FITness in action. Central to the theory is the role played by *feedback* in changing the way the person responds as a consequence of their previous experiences. They propose that human behaviour can be characterized as a self-regulating system with four component parts:

- The presence of a *goal, standard of comparison,* or *reference* values against which to consider your actions and decisions. In FIT theory this is explicitly Integrity and the five Constancies.

- The perception or *monitoring* of the effects of your actions and decisions. In FIT this role is played by the Awareness Constancy. It is our contention that many people do not self-regulate anything like as much as they should because they are hardly ever aware, except in a vague sense and having their eyes open.

- The *comparison* with the reference values, of the information received from monitoring. Awareness is central here too.

- A *corrective adjustment* to be made to future decisions and behaviours if there is a discrepancy present when the comparator stage is executed. Commitment to change is necessary. Many people do not actually make such self-regulated changes either because they do not have commitment to the reference goals themselves (because they are not explicit or clear enough), or because they lack the necessary motivation to change. FIT contains its own self-motivating values.

FIT theory proposes that self-improvement is likely at each of these stages in the regulatory system. FIT is explicitly a cognitive self-regulating theory, where the commitment to change for the future is a built-in aspect of it. One advantage of FIT is that it minimizes the likelihood that people will use the wrong kind of feedback in making self-corrections in what they do. This is a common problem which is the root of much misplaced behaviour. For example, people are apt to place considerable reliance on random factors or superstitious beliefs that play a major role in decisions and behaviours (from doing the lottery, having lucky charms, to walking around ladders). These often have innocuous consequences, but neurotic and psychotic behaviours also have them as their bedrock causes. Such superstitions and random factors bias a great deal of the behaviour of ordinary people. FIT theory has a firm foundation in the real world because it encourages a more realistic assessment of the internal and external environments by the individual. It makes it more likely that the person will use their self-directed attentional processes to use the feedback they receive, to engage the comparator, and to make adjustments. Professors Carver and Schier have done a considerable amount of research to show that self-directed attention, and the use of feedback, makes people change what they do. They have shown that having standards against which to compare actions and decisions is essential. FIT is not just a theory – it is a theory that can work.

Having control

One of the biggest stressors, which influences both individual and organizational well-being and performance, is lack of control, lack of discretion, or low levels of autonomy. It has been shown, especially in the work context, that people with higher levels of control can cope much better with high work demands. Indeed they may even thrive on them. Work environments that do not allow sufficient discretion are dangerous to psychological and physical health. The FIT perspective would predict that thwarted attempts at keeping personal control (in some part of a person's environment) would produce negative outcomes, especially in a dynamic and demanding environment. FIT, though, implies more than this. It suggests, for example, that FITter individuals will seek more potential control but will be less affected by the lack of environmental control, since they will find ways of obviating the constraints. FITter individuals will also respond more to being given greater discretion (their 'growth need strength' is greater). They have more potential too. The FIT will be in control, or take it where possible, while the unFIT will be open to the vagaries and apparently random influences of the outside or environmental factors. We have some evidence for this assertion. In our early empirical studies we have found that the FITter individuals perceive fewer constraints in their work environment, are less affected by lower levels of job discretion and have lower levels of anxiety and depression, compared to less FIT individuals.

Personality theory

FIT theory is concerned with providing a different kind of vocabulary for describing differences between individuals. In one sense it is a personality theory. However, it goes much further than a personality theory because it also offers explicit criteria for personal development and success: it both characterizes people in terms of FITness and implies what individuals must do to be more successful and psychologically healthy. Psychological health and well-being should be an individual and organizational goal for everyone and every organization, if only for the health and efficiency gains it entails.

The FIT theory makes a number of predictions that set it quite apart from other theories of individual differences and personal development. Perhaps the most marked of these concerns the relationship between observed behaviours and the inferences about the individual (in terms of FITness) that can be made. In FIT theory it makes no sense to talk of 'personality traits', or different 'personality types', even if such things may have a reality. What matters is the degree to which a person is FIT. If two individuals were '100 percent FIT' they would be indistinguishable in terms of their behaviours. A FIT person does not have a personality (in the behavioural sense of acting inappropriately). FITness, or appropriateness of behaviour, would distinguish between people, and not some imprisoned, inherited or acquired behavioural tendency or reaction. In traditional theories of personality the emphasis of the theory is on the dominant or invariant aspects of behaviour or inner state. These propose that one can infer something about the nature of the personality traits or states of the individual from the similarities in their behaviour, or consistency of reactions, across different circumstances. These inferences can be made from direct observation or indirectly (as is usual) from self-report questionnaires or personality tests.

Although some psychologists view traits as social constructions of individuals arising out of the need for them to communicate self-identity, the 'existence' of traits has seen something of a renaissance in the 1990s. In general, it appears that people can be classified along a few dimensions that are common for all. The most commonly accepted split is into what are known as 'the Big Five' personality variables:

- Extroversion

- Neuroticism

- Openness

- Agreeableness, and

- Conscientiousness

Some very well known personality tests have more than five dimensions. One of the world's most widely used is Cattell's 16PF series of tests, named after its originator Professor Raymond Cattell. The '16PF' is shorthand for 16 primary personality factors, which are:

- Outgoing

- Abstract thinking

- Emotional stability

- Assertiveness

- Enthusiasm

- Conscientiousness

- Sociability

- Tough-mindedness

- Trust

- Practicality

- Astuteness

- Self-assuredness

- Experimenting

- Self-sufficiency

- Control

- Relaxed

- and the additional 'lie-type' scale of Impression Management

Using various statistical techniques these 16 can be distilled to five global dimensions – the Big Five (above).

In personality theory there has been considerable debate over whether such 'traits' provide a meaningful role in predicting behaviour. Some researchers have suggested that behaviour is so variable and unreliable across different situations that the concept of traits provides no worthwhile predictiveness and should be abandoned in favour of a situationalist perspective in which the situation, not the personality, determines the behaviour displayed by the individual. There has been much written on this 'person–situation' debate and the sense of an 'interactionist' perspective which tries to encompass both by demonstrating that behaviour is a function of both the personality of the individual and the type of situation they are in. Such views, which appear at one level to be entirely sensible, preserve the need for traits that do play a causal role in how a person behaves despite the contextual dependency of their operation.

For some personality theories, the inner states (or the 'phenomenological experience' of the person) may be different for the same set of behavioural circumstances. For some theorists the same behaviour can have very different underlying personal experiences. For example, the *Reversal Theory* of Michael Apter (1997), which Apter himself considers 'radical', rejects the view that people operate homeostatically, or in terms of a single stable situation. It suggests that people can be 'multistable' inasmuch as they switch (or reverse) from one structural or 'metamotivational' state to another without any change in environmental circumstances. For Apter, for example, the same level of arousal or the same environmental demands can produce apparently contradictory feelings at different times in the same person – excitement or fright, boredom or relaxation.

For each of these classes of theory the essence of the theory is derived from the consistency (or observable predictability) of the hypothesized personality variable, however that is conceptualized (i.e. as a trait, phenomenological structure, interactionist outcome). This predictability is, of course, at the very core of methodology in the field of psychology. The concept of FIT suggests an alternative. According to FIT theory the essence, in behavioural terms, is of behavioural flexibility, not of behaviour constrained by predominant structural tendencies. The FIT person behaves according to the demands of the situation (based on the five Constancies) and is not captured by history, their traits, or any other inherent tendency. FIT is not, however, a 'situationalist' theory because FIT behaviour is very much determined by the individual. The behaviour is ideally personal, and not situational, inasmuch as it should raise their level of Integrity and not, in some external sense, be 'the right thing to do' or 'the best decision' (although it should be from an individual perspective). Indeed, according to FIT, the FITter the person is (i.e. the more they operate in terms of the Constancies), the less obvious their patterns of behaviour which are the usual building blocks of personality theories. An unFIT person will be revealed by their consistency across different environments and the way in which they will behave in a similar manner to the way they did in the past, however inappropriate this is.

This difference can be put in a different way. If one were to crudely label the personal drivers or motivators of individuals according to the different classes of personality theory these might be as follows:

Trait/Dominance theories	The structure of traits, hard-wired behaviours
Situationalists/Reversal theory	Phenomenological experience/ current feelings; environmental demands; needs
FIT	the Constancy Equation; Integrity; 'I'

Only FIT theory would predict that individuals who feel the same might behave differently – other stances would attribute this to measurement error. FIT theory also differs from others inasmuch as it classifies individuals along a single continuum (FITness), rather than on a number of independent variables or traits which share (by definition) no common root. Classification conundrum and infinite predictive complexity can easily obscure in multi-factor models, and provide a strong defence against falsification.

Personality traits and ability

In the main, personality traits and ability (e.g. intelligence) are considered separately. This is because the definition of a personality trait is meant to be uncontaminated by ability measures, according to psychologists, since they are fundamentally meant to be different kinds of construct. For example, one of the 'Big Five' traits, *Openness to Experience*, is statistically correlated, or associated, to intelligence and divergent thinking ability – both ability measures. The implication of a trait being dependent on ability leads some psychologists to the conclusion that it cannot be considered a true personality trait.

FIT theory is indifferent to such issues, even if it was true that FITness and ability measures were associated, such that those with higher ability may have more potential for FITness. What matters for FIT is appropriateness of behaviour to the situation; not stereotypic or dominant behavioural patterns which are not responsive to the situation. In this sense, the personality of the individual should be subsumed to, or consumed by, the context of the situation.

Performance and success

The status of personality traits is compromised further by the findings that, in the main, even the best personality tests are very poor predictors, if at all, of job performance. An ex-colleague, Dr Steve Blinkhorn (and Steve Johnson) demonstrated this in a scientific paper in 1990. Why are personality tests used so much in selection and assessment? FITness assessments would be much more relevant. FITness is highly related to success and performance – especially in companies which allow individuals autonomy, which have systems that support FIT people, where work is appropriately designed, and which operate ethically and morally. The 1990s cry of HR departments – to align the goals of the individual and the organization to get the most out of them – would be even more loudly hailed in this context. The benefits of FITness, both in human and economic terms, would be enormous.

The real self and personal integrity

'The genius of Freud lay in his awareness of the importance of the unconscious, including its capacity for distorting the operation of the higher mental processes. It follows that human reasoning is not nearly as rational as most people wish to believe' (Seymour Epstein, 1997: 18–19). For many psychotherapists a person's true identity or real self is somehow hidden by the masks they learn to wear, often inappropriately or dysfunctionally. For Jungian psychoanalysts the 'persona' is the mask of the self that is displayed to the outside world. It follows that in order to 'find oneself' this view proposes that one must strip away all the layers of learned self-deceit, all the neuroses, all the powerful influences from the past, and all the ill-fitting responses and behaviours that hide the true self. The large number of psychotherapists and counsellors is testament to the appeal of this approach, even forgetting the more esoteric movements devoted to similar and related ends.

Such an approach would be anathema within the context of FIT. The 'true self' is not an historical past locked in layers of experience which need expunging – it is not some kind of residual core. Rather, it is one's potential; it is defined by what is possible, by future options and successes instead of past failures. The individual is defined by how FIT they are and what FITness capacity they may have. FIT theory is forward-looking without barriers to growth, not an historical past in search of a personal key. FITness does *not* say 'go with your spirit' – which is rather free and easy and allows for all manner of immoral and unacceptable behaviours – but 'go with your Integrity' which may be very different and possibly effortful. We often need to do the opposite of what we feel.

There has been interesting related research looking at the relationship between the personal projects that people engage in and what they get out of them in terms of happiness and meaning. Professor Brian Little, from Carleton University in the USA, has pioneered what he calls *Personal Projects Analysis* (PPA) in an attempt to investigate whether 'being yourself' has benefits for well-being, in addition to the established link between personal success or effectiveness and feeling good. 'Personal projects' are the sorts of things everyone has. They are individual to the person but reflect something about them, their values and what they find important to actually do, including such things as 'floss teeth regularly', 'lose weight', 'help the poor', 'travel to the Far East', 'phone parents each week' and 'support partner more'. People can usually list 14 or 15 such personal projects at any one time. In some sense these projects reflect the identity of the person over time in all their various guises and contexts. Professor Little suggests that the integrity of the person can be inferred from how consistent the personal projects are with one's core identity and that this can be revealed by how meaningful they are seen to be by the individual.

In a journal article in the *Journal of Personality and Social Psychology* in 1998, (74(2): 494–512) Little reports two studies designed to see if well-being was related to personal integrity as well as personal efficacy or success. A strong link was found between the perceived meaningfulness of personal projects and personal integrity. The success which people felt about their personal projects was also clearly a determinant of their happiness. In general, the meaningfulness of their personal projects was associated with measures of personal growth, purpose in life and relationships and felt autonomy or independence, while (un)happiness was a determinant of stress, depression and life dissatisfaction.

The research also revealed that personal integrity was partly responsible for the link between happiness and meaning got from the projects. The people who had personal projects that were consistent with the core elements of their self-identity reported higher levels of meaning and were happier than those with less integration. Professor Little suggests that this is because felt efficacy probably acts as a surrogate for personal integrity in the earlier stages of life, or when one has not yet experienced success in life. He shows that there is an 'integrity shift' which occurs with successful managers who do not display the association between efficacy and well-being, although personal integrity and well-being are strongly linked. As the researchers say the 'sole reliance on efficacy might not be a prudent well-being strategy ... using efficacy as a surrogate for integrity in early life might leave one vulnerable to despair in later life' (p. 508).

Personal potential

A strength of the FIT theory is its emphasis on personal potential. FITness is not just a descriptive theory but can also be said to have evaluative connotations. It makes no real sense to talk about the need for individuals to become more extrovert, or neurotic, less achievement oriented or alloic: the theory, whatever it is, is meant merely as a descriptive and predictive device. FITness, however, is a potential all have but only some will begin to realize. It is also something that confers benefit to the individual. Abraham Maslow in his seminal book *Motivation and Personality*, published in 1954, had much to say about the value of this aspect of theory when contrasting his own theory of motivation with traditional approaches. For example, he writes, 'We are now able to judge the essential nature of humans in terms of what their possibilities, potentialities, and highest possible development may be, instead of relying only on external observations of what is the case at this moment. This approach sums up to this: History has practically always sold human nature short' (p. 116).

According to FIT theory, therefore, it is not possible to predict FITness from the similarities in behaviour across similar or different circumstances, except perhaps by the degree to which the behaviours can be attributed to the residual personal histories, which may obviate against FITness. It is, therefore, important, both at an individual and theory level, to be able to provide criteria against which FITness can be measured.

FITness could be seen as sharing many of the benefits Maslow attributed to 'self-actualizing people' (those who fully exploited their talents, capacities and potentialities and could, therefore, be called 'healthy'). Maslow intended to study such people with reference to a sample of 3000 college students. However, his screening criteria produced no self-actualizers at all. Nor could he find any such figures from the figures created by novelists and playwrights. He had to be content with a study of several historical figures (which included Albert Einstein, William James and Albert Schweitzer) and some of his contemporaries whom he considered also fell some way short of self-actualization (Is this analogous to the generally low mean FIT scores we observe? All appear to have considerable potential). He found that there were a number of things that this sample had in common, including:

- an ability to perceive things for what they are (less partial than others);

- acceptance of their situation without anxiety or guilt;

- spontaneity of behaviour with marked simplicity and naturalness;

- a focus on problems outside themselves;

- greater solitude or healthy detachment from others;

- relative independence and autonomy from their environment;

- a fresh appreciation in the repetition of things;

- peak or intensive experiences, including mystical ones;

- kinship or affection for others, including deeper interpersonal relationships;

- humility and respect for others;

- an ethical appreciation of right and wrong with firm values;

- creativity;

- a resistance to enculturation without rebellion;

- imperfections and mistakes;

- the resolution of dichotomies or polarities (they are both, for example, ruthlessly selfish and unselfish, concrete and abstract, etc.).

This last aspect is particularly important in the context of FITness because the existence of apparently conflicting behaviours at different times is an integral part of the concept of behaving appropriately and flexibly. Maslow writes:

The dichotomy between selfishness and unselfishness disappears altogether in healthy people because in principle every act is both selfish and unselfish. Our subjects are simultaneously very spiritual and very pagan and sensual . . . duty is pleasure . . . work is play . . . the most mature are also childlike. . . . Similar findings have been reached for kindness–ruthlessness, concreteness–abstractness, acceptance–rebellion, self–society, adjustment–maladjustment, detachment from others–identification with others, serious–humorous, Dionysian–Appolanian, introverted–extroverted, intense–casual, serious-frivolous, conventional–unconventional, mystic–realistic, active-passive, masculine–feminine. . . . In these people, the id, the ego, and the superego are collaborative and synergistic; they do not war with each other . . . the higher and the lower are not in opposition but in agreement, and a thousand serious philosophical dilemmas are discovered to have more than two horns or, paradoxically, no horns at all. (p. 149)

The effects of environmental constraints and stressful experiences

There has been a considerable amount of research on such topics as childhood abuse, the effects of major life traumas and events, the influence of previous (often childhood) experiences, occupational stress, post-traumatic stress syndrome, and the effects of acute or distressing events and bad experiences. Research considers both the immediate psychological and bodily effects as well as the likely consequences of the difficulties over time. Negative effects are commonly hypothesized and are found to be pernicious and often long lasting, as well as difficult to extinguish. The study of work stress, to take an example, has become complex, with the need for theoretically driven research, objective indicators of stressors and strains, the need to take account of individual differences and the use of sophisticated statistical modelling tools. Emphasis is on examining the effects of changes in the work environment. Effects of work stressors have been shown to be acute as well as chronic in their action, psychological, physiological and disease-related, to depend upon various individual variables (such as hardiness, positive spirit, Type A characteristics), and to influence those not directly exposed to the stressors via psychological mechanisms. These aspects were reviewed in a previous book by Professor Fletcher entitled *Work, Stress, Disease and Life Expectancy*, published in 1991.

What can the FIT perspective contribute to these debates? FIT theory does not take issue with the findings of such research. On the contrary, much has been achieved by this kind of research. To take one example from the study of work stress, it is now well established that it makes no sense to look at particular work stressors in isolation and to show how people negatively perceive these. What people report does not reflect either the causes of stress or often any kind of problem for them. People often cannot say with any reality whether or not they are suffering strain. We have seen, for example, many people working too many hours who have no insight into the injurious consequences they are showing, nor the costs in terms of their lost efficiency. On the contrary, such workaholics will vigorously defend their health and work practices. We now know that how people respond to work stressors is greatly affected by the totality of their situation, including their coping processes, their domestic situation, their individuality and many other factors. Life does not come wrapped up in separate independent boxes. Sometimes it only takes an apparently insignificant problem or stressor to flip a person into being very stressed, and previously enjoyable experiences can become negative – having a coffee break or going to the gym can be difficult to cope with when the negative flip has occurred. This has been captured in Professor Fletcher's *Catastrophe Theory of Stress*, which describes the mechanisms involved, and how, once over the stressful threshold, the negative flip, or catastrophe, causes a complete change in how people see and respond to their environment. That is one reason the world of the stressed person is very different from the world of the unstressed person.

Part of that Catastrophe Theory was also the idea that other contextual aspects of stress are important. For example, the effects of any stressor needs to be viewed not in isolation, but in terms of the overall balance of *Demands, Supports and Constraints* in which strain is the result of the lack of balance between three work factors:

- *Job demands:* This is the degree to which the work environment contains stimuli which peremptorily require attention and response. The demands might be technical, intellectual, social and financial. Job demands are the things that have to be done and the environment in which the individual is placed. Table 8.2 presents some common job demands.

- *Job supports:* This is the degree to which the work environment contains available resources that are relevant to the demands of the individual or the group. These supports may be technical, intellectual, social, financial, etc. For example, being part of a happy cohesive workforce may make the job demands easier to cope with. It is important to note that support does not simply refer to social or interpersonal aspects, although these are known to reduce the effects of stress. It also includes such job factors as being clear about the task in hand and having a measure of autonomy and discretion over how the work is ordered and executed.

■ *Job constraints:* Jobs are made much harder by the lack of relevant resources which are usually finite in supply. Such constraints can act to prevent the individual maximizing the benefits of the supports, as well as affect how they can cope with the demands. Thus constraints are those aspects of the working environment which prevent the worker or group from coping with the demands. Table 8.2 shows some common supports-constraints (for operational reasons, supports and constraints are treated as a single dimension).

TABLE 8.2 Work stressors as demands or supports-constraints (taken from Fletcher, 1991)

Work demands	Work supports-constraints
Job pressure	Being clear about role
Having too much to do	Job discretion, autonomy or control
Having too little to do	Quality of relationships with:
Being responsible for people	Boss
Responsibility for things (equipment)	Colleagues
Demands from others	Subordinates
Conflicting demands/roles	Union membership
Over/under promotion	Role ambiguity
Keeping up with others/organizations	Variety level/skill utilization
Organizational climate	Social perception of job
Office politics	Participation in decisions
Organizational structure	Payment/reward system
Organizational/job changes	Quality of equipment
Major decisions	Physical working conditions
Expectancies of others/organization	How work is planned/managed

According to the Demands-Supports-Constraints model of stress, strain results from a lack of balance between the three variables. Thus, high job demands are not stressful (i.e. they do not lead to strain) if the job also provides good levels of support and low constraints. In fact, high demands can be positively good in the right circumstances because they provide stimulation and utilize the worker's abilities – underutilization of abilities and boredom are amongst the most potent stressors and also usually occur in work environments where supports are low and constraints high. One obvious practical implication of the model is that highly demanding jobs can be made less stressful without reducing the level of the demands: instead the level of supports can be increased or the constraints reduced. The model has implications for redesigning work to reduce the amount of strain in an organization whilst at the same time boosting efficiency.

FIT theory develops this type of research in a different direction, while at the same time utilizing the important lessons from it. In the context of FIT theory, the more FIT people are, and the more of them there are in the particular group being studied, the less likely it is that traditional approaches in stress research will reveal any useful or meaningful links and explanations. The FITter people will be aware of the important environmental dimensions, but will not be as affected negatively by them. It is not that FIT people do not experience the stressors, but it is the way that they deal with them that sets them apart. The environment is potentially stressful for the FIT and the unFIT alike. However, unFIT people find themselves engulfed by the world and their own ineffective histories, and will succumb to strains through the high constraints and negative interpretations implied in such a situation. FIT people, on the other hand, base their behaviour and decisions on the 'Constancies equation'. This means they will not, therefore, be affected in a negative way because they have taken responsibility for the state of affairs, are aware of the various options and alternatives, and have a properly evaluated personal position (i.e. their FIT *Integrity* is high). The traditional stress research findings are only applicable to the unFIT, and the models derived from them – they are only useful in this negative way. In terms of FIT theory, chronic effects of stress occur because unFIT people fail many times to deal with a recurrent situation. The unFIT fail to learn from this past and to change their decisions and behaviours.

Stress management techniques will also be of only potential short-term benefit to the unFIT unless they positively change the evaluation of their situation in FIT-related ways. What is needed is a study of stress from the alternative – the FIT – perspective.

The inconsistencies in human behaviour

The research on occupational stress shows us quite clearly that people are far from consistent in their behaviours or attributions, and that they vary day by day in terms of how they react. The inconsistency of human behaviour is probably what sets it apart from the behaviour of other animals. People have a propensity to change their minds, to act on a whim, to do silly things, to do the unpredicted. People have irrational fears and superstitions of which they are fully aware. They have many others of which they are not aware. They will make decisions they know not to be sensible, logical or rational. They will argue a position in the face of overwhelming evidence to the contrary, and will allow themselves and others to do things that are immoral, personally and socially damaging, and environmentally compromising. Different kinds of models have been generated to account for such inconsistencies. The majority of these imply that such inconsistencies arise from the tensions and changing predominances of multiple (usually dual) underlying systems. For Sigmund Freud these were the unconscious 'primary process' and the more conscious and rational 'secondary process'. He saw rational overt behaviour as being influenced and distorted considerably by the long-imprisoned wish fulfilment processes. One major problem with this conceptualization is that the unconscious processes posited by Freud are not adaptive from an evolutionary perspective despite their primary role in human behaviour. Indeed, they are very maladaptive and destructive.

In an attempt to overcome this problem Seymour Epstein (1994) has developed what he calls *Cognitive-Experiential Self-Theory* (CEST) in which it is proposed that people construct their own theory of the world based on explicit and implicit beliefs and schema. Humans, but not other animals, also develop a self-theory. These constructs – of the world and the self – are developed and controlled by two opposing mechanisms which Epstein calls the 'experiential' and the 'rational' systems. The joint operations of these two systems control all behaviour. The experiential system – based on experience and personal history – operates largely unconsciously, automatically, holistically, non-verbally, rapidly, passively, stereotypically and emotionally, but is slow to change and to integrate the new. The rational system operates without taking account of personal histories. It is logical, analytic, conscious and context-independent and can change with the speed of a thought without the need for experience (only evidence). Rational and consistent decisions are interfered with by four experiential system demands: to maximize pleasure–pain balance, to maintain a stable model, to maintain relatedness, and to enhance self-esteem. There is an impressive body of evidence in support of the CEST notion covering a whole range of contexts from heuristic reasoning experiments, social processes, psychotherapy, personality measurement and clinical practice. CEST predicts why we often say one thing and do another, or why our emotions sometimes dramatically affect our logic and rational behaviour.

CEST posits that the experiential system operates in parallel with the rational system to determine behaviour. In some sense, history combats logic for the victory to control decision making. Considered intentions will influence outcome through the part they would play in the rational channels. For FIT theory this system is too static, although it may well predict outcomes in the unFIT. FIT provides for an ongoing monitoring and dynamic change to the outputs of such static systems. The Constancies provide individuals with explicit guidelines against which to compare all behaviours, verbal and otherwise. FIT also posits that awareness at many levels can provide information to inform possible actions. FITness takes it as axiomatic that the FIT person will not be seduced by their history (or the output of a CEST system). They take responsibility to construct a personal *'behaviour-future'* which is dynamically controlled (albeit with automatic sub-units of output which do not require constant attention), and which can operate independently of emotion and logic. It is important to realize that, according to FITness, rationality should not always win. The FIT person is an emotional person when the situation demands it, a rational one when the situation demands it – the situation together with the personal Constancies dictates, not the CEST-type processing systems.

One could view aspects of the FIT framework in terms of the distinction between rational and experiential dimensions. Integrity (the 'output' of the five Constancies) could be said to be composed of rational imperatives (to maintain balance, self-responsibility, and morality) and experiential ones (fearlessness), together with a monitoring mechanism to achieve this (awareness). In this sense, the FIT framework integrates the emotional and rational dimensions.

The disconnection between intentions, feelings and behaviours

It has long been known that people's espoused attitudes and their behaviours do not appear to correspond. Early research on racial prejudice, for example, demonstrated that people would state quite definitely that they were not prejudiced, but their observed behaviours showed quite the opposite. Changes in opinion that do occur, despite the internal need for stability, are often not translated into behaviour.

Research has also demonstrated that there is a disconnection between what people know and how well they can do things. For example, an American experimental psychologist, Arthur Reber, has shown that people may learn very complex abstract rules without being aware, so that they can subsequently make decisions which require knowledge of the rules but have no explicit knowledge of what the rules are. This is called 'implicit learning' and has been shown to apply to many types of situation, including economic decision making, factory production models and even social interaction with others. When people are told to try to discern what the rules are – to 'explicitly learn' – this interferes markedly with how well they can learn and the strategies they adopt. The implications of such work are far reaching for education and training, but the point to note here is the degree of dislocation they imply between what people think and do.

There has also been interesting work to see if the quality of experience, how good people feel, is related to what they actually do. One might expect leisure time, for example, to provide people with more 'optimal experiences' and less aversive experiences than when they are at work. Optimal experiences are those involving voluntary attention focusing, whereas aversive ones are those which are involuntary or dictated. Milahly Csikszentmihalyi calls optimal experience 'flow'. Csikszentmihalyi and Judith LeFevre (1989) studied 78 adults for one week to see if this was so. They used an interesting method in which the quality of people's experiences was randomly sampled at any time of the day through contact via 'beepers' or electronic paging devices. When beeped the people had to drop what they were doing to complete a simple structured self-report form about what they were doing and how they felt. Previous work had shown that people feel more active, alert, concentrated, happy, satisfied, creative and generally more positive when challenges and skill needs are high but balanced. Surprisingly, the researchers found that there were three times more flow experiences during work compared to leisure time when people were supposed to be enjoying themselves. This was true for blue-collar workers as well as managers. When not at work people spent more than 10 percent of their leisure time watching television despite the fact that they themselves reported about two-thirds of that time that they did not feel flow, but boredom, apathy or anxiety. It seems that people say they do not want to be at work but actually get excitement and fulfilment while doing it, say they would rather be doing something else, but then do something that they do not find enjoyable.

Such inconsistencies between what people feel yet do are common. Other examples include smoking, some eating disorders, alcoholism and other cases of 'addiction' which do not appear to have any obvious biological basis such as nailbiting, compulsive cleanliness, workaholism, shopaholic behaviour and other behavioural compulsions. In most cases the person is aware of their condition, would rather not be run by the compulsion, yet appears unable to break the bad behavioural cycle.

FIT people are connected with their inner feelings and are, therefore, more predictable and consistent (if the situation is adequately understood). They do what is appropriate, not what the vagaries of their personal history dictates.

The unconscious, the black holes of the mind, and FITness

Unconscious processes are learned. Unconsciousness is a construction of past factors. The unconscious influences are one way in which the past has its dirty way on what people do now. The unconscious is like a black hole that sucks in experiences and personal influences without us noticing. It stops people from being their conscious selves and from doing what they would otherwise intend. In some sense it sucks the mind from people. It stops people from responding appropriately. Black holes are very powerful in their influence on all matter close to them – so too the black holes of the mind. FITness provides a tool with which to resist the pull of the black hole. Some people have very large black holes and these cannot be resisted or repaired easily. The FIT are less likely to be affected by the unconscious influences (which are derived from the past) because they are guided more by the Constancies than that past.

Social factors in FITness

The essence of FIT is in the potential of individuals, not the current state of affairs. All people have the same potential to FITness, although not all have had the vocabulary or experiences to aspire to it. A central aspect of FITness is the ability to behave appropriately and not in a constrained stereotypical manner. This is true in all contexts, in all social circumstances. If a person is from a 'lower' social class they can demonstrate FITness in that environment, if they behave according to the Constancies. They may not know all the rules for new contexts, but will be quick to learn them. The unFIT from a 'higher' class will not behave appropriately in a 'lower' context, nor will they learn any new rules very quickly. The unFIT find it more difficult to cross social or other boundaries and stereotypes, but the FIT person has no such boundaries, even if their current life circumstances are constrained. FITness will be independent of social class. The FIT may be an elite, but FITness is not elitist.

FIT: advantages over other approaches

The advantages of the FIT approach

The FIT approach is distinctive because it attempts to provide a broad understanding of behaviour and of decision-making processes, as well as the underlying mechanisms that are responsible for them.

FIT also begins from the view that an individual's personal history does not have to dictate how that person responds and develops. That is, FIT breaks the learning-history mould. History is a strong mould and one that exists for good reason. FIT is another perspective. It begins from the point of potential, not past (which is also its disadvantage). For example, if we were trying to determine how a person would cope with a potentially stressful job, the FIT approach would not begin by a measurement of the stressors and demands in the job, nor would it look first at the person's past responses. It begins from a determination of the individual's level of FITness now: that is the predictor. FIT provides a stance which begins by jettisoning the past and looking at the now.

FIT does not penalize people for their past behaviour habits, nor presume that bad external environments need have negative effects on people. Two examples might help to explain what is meant here. First, it is a common belief that if people have failed or made mistakes and errors before they are more likely to do so again. This may be true, but FITness would prevent it from happening. Second, it may also be true that a stressful work environment will generally produce low job satisfaction and illness. But this is not the whole picture. FIT proposes that individuals should use their learning in making their decisions, but should not be imprisoned by that learning. The FIT person would experience the work environment, but their Integrity would protect them from the negative consequences of it and also ensure corrective and protective actions were taken.

The FIT view states that using the past as predictors may be statistically sound, but ignores the error that will be made in doing so. The fallacy that a statistical link is a casual one is well known (a correlation between the number of priests and increases in paedophilia does not imply any link at all), but FITness is saying something more. The FIT approach asks that the past–future links need to be weighed against the errors of such predictions together with the value of using just now–future predictive power. FIT tries to shift the emphasis to making analyses work forwards from the now. It suggests that if the starting points are in the past then the systems (the person, or whatever system is being predicted – such as money markets, horse racing, and the economy) have an in-built failure, which will be directly proportional to the extent that that past is imperfect. An economic system or a money market cannot be FIT (although the analysis of it can be), but people can try to be. FIT theory begins from the axiomatic point that proper analysis of the current state and future pointers must be more predictive than basing predictions on historical analyses. Historical analyses were appropriate to a very different set of circumstances and time. Now is different. Future will be more so. Therefore, the FIT approach must be more fruitful and accurate. FIT provides a context for future prediction which begins from the current position of the person, without the potential error of including their past baggage. The FIT perspective puts the past in context, uses it, but does not allow it more influence than it deserves. FIT tries to get out of reverse gear.

Another example to illustrate this difference may be useful. It is well known that people show considerable variability in their behaviours at different times, even in circumstances that look similar. It is also accepted that they show some similarities in how they react, even in different circumstances. This is one reason psychologists have developed the idea that people can be categorized in terms of personality traits. In terms of FIT theory, the personality trait is a concept that 'freezes' personal history. Any failure in the trait concept is due to errors of measurement or the lack of refinement in the description of the trait itself. To put it another way, the lack of predictability is due to error. However, the variability in behaviours is to be expected in FIT theory. If the person is FIT they will be sensitive to the nuances in the situation. If they are unFIT, it is due to their reliance on those traits (personal history) which provide inappropriate guidance for the situation the person is in. FIT provides an understanding of situation-specific behaviour that accounts for person-specific characteristics. It provides a personal growth framework, which can be individual, and one that takes full account of internal as well as external criteria.

The FIT framework provides moment-by-moment criteria for choice (the Constancies and Integrity). It also provides long-term goals – to be aware and become FIT, for example. That is, it does provide a context for personal development but with short-term aids or constant reminders. Many personal development tools do not include such guidance templates, but concentrate on visions and missions being integrated into normal patterns of behaviour.

The emphasis in FIT is on the individual. People are seen as responsible for their own states and therefore, the events that occur. In a sense this puts a new tilt on the ideas of empowerment and personal responsibility which are champions of modern movements in work design and good management practice. FIT widens this context even further. People are responsible for themselves, their work, their relationships and their wider social and economic conditions. If changes are needed in these areas, the start should come from the individuals' state or thoughts.

FIT provides for an exciting and adventurous world with potential and possibility rather than constraint and limitation. It attempts to bring back some individual magic. For example, it provides an internal justification for someone to enlarge the normal range of their behaviours and to increase their behavioural flexibility, thus allowing greater enjoyment from an enlarged realm of experience. People are encouraged to enter their discomfort zones and learn new and enhanced personal horizons. Potential is enjoyable. It becomes the norm – and comfortable.

A summary of some of the advantages of the FIT approach is given in Figure 9.1.

Psychotherapy, counselling, behavioural and cognitive therapies

There are many people who have psychological problems. We know, for example, that around 10 percent of the so-called 'healthy' working population will have clinically relevant levels of anxiety or depression, with a further 20 percent at marginal levels. These are people with problems they often cannot solve for themselves but who do not always get professional help. It may be that FITness would be helpful for them, but that is not its intention. There are more than 400 systems of therapy available to help those with psychological dysfunction. They all provide a model or theory of human behaviour that acts as the framework for the intervention of the therapist or counsellor. In general, they all attempt the same thing: to get at, and examine, the core beliefs of the individual

FIGURE 9.1   The advantages of the FIT approach

FIT breaks the learning-history mould. The prisoner is freed.

It begins from the point of potential not past (which is also its disadvantage).

It is not based on an 'error-by-default' approach.

FIT provides an understanding of situation-specific behaviour which accounts for person-specific characteristics.

FIT provides a context for long-term personal development but with short-term aids or constant reminders (i.e. the Constancies).

The emphasis in FIT is on the individual. People are seen as responsible for their own states and therefore, the events that occur.

FIT provides for an exciting and adventurous world with potential and possibility rather than constraint and limitation. Potential is enjoyable.

FIT has a theoretical underpinning. It is not based on a 'cookbook' or haphazard approach.

FIT is not a 'therapy' – it is useful for everyone.

---

and where they come from, with a view to reformulating them so that the person is better adjusted. Some of the main therapeutic categories are:

■   Primary medical and psychiatric assistance, which usually treats with drugs, or via referral to one of the other groups, or uses treatments of the kind, listed below.

■   Counselling and psychotherapy, of which there are many types with differing traditions and techniques. There are the psychoanalytic traditions of Freud and Jung and the neo-Freudians and neo-Jungians. There is Rogerian, Eriksonian and family-based counselling. There are other approaches such as Brief Focal Psychotherapy, pioneered by Professor Malan, which looks at the key issues in smaller packets than other approaches. There is Interpersonal Psychotherapy (IPP) which focuses on significant others in the well-being of the individual. There are Gestalt approaches which remain fashionable in some countries and with some therapists.

■   Behavioural therapies, where the emphasis is on changing a person's responses to difficult situations with various reward-based or desensitizing routines, in the belief that changes in thoughts and feeling will soon follow.

- Some of the different approaches are combined for maximal effect. Perhaps the best known is Cognitive Behavioural Therapy, or CBT, which looks for the thoughts that trigger the negative emotions. Personal Construct Psychotherapy looks at the underlying structures of thoughts and behaviours and attempts to provide more functional constructs to guide behaviour. Cognitive Analytic Therapies, or CAT, borrow intervention techniques from a wide range of approaches, depending upon the patient's problems. The emphasis is on changing the perception of situations that have hitherto been threatening, or helping to provide a cognitive perspective that more closely accords with the way most people see things.

With some of the therapies it has been shown that individualized professional assistance is not always required to effect beneficial changes. Group-based help, or indeed written materials (called bibliotherapy), can also be effective in reducing clinical symptoms of physical and psychological illness. In one study done by a PhD student of Professor Fletcher's, Gary Kupshik, himself a high-grade clinical psychologist, showed that people with low mood or anxiety who were referred by their GPs showed marked symptom relief with an assisted bibliotherapy programme. The significance of such research is that it shows that people who do not go to their doctor for help with these psychological problems may show symptom relief if they are given access to such materials. This is important for three reasons. First, given the high cost of primary medical psychological services, bibliotherapy is very cost-effective and can, therefore, be made more widely available. Second, only a small proportion of those needing psychological help try to get it from formal sources. Only about 20 percent of those with depression or anxiety discuss this with their doctor. Bibliotherapy may reduce some of the resistance to getting help. Third, primary medical services may promote 'sick role behaviours' not associated with bibliotherapy.

In recent years there has been considerable debate over the effectiveness of some clinical approaches. Various researchers have argued that some of the techniques do more harm than good, especially those involving personal therapists and counsellors outside the governance of the medical context. Psychodynamic therapy, in particular, has been the subject of much discussion in this regard. Others argue that any benefit, however achieved, however transient, and however individual, is of value.

Common to many of the counselling and psychotherapeutic approaches is that they look for answers in the person's past. This is anathema to the FIT approach where the emphasis is not on the past causes of behaviour, nor even the structure of cognitions, but on the contemporaneous use of templates (the Constancies) to guide behaviour and decisions. The future fits into place with these ongoing decisions. The past should be irrelevant (but people do find it difficult to release themselves from past behaviour habits and thoughts). Therapies usually take significant numbers of sessions to begin to be effective. FITness may also take time, but there is no structural reason why it should: the central ideas are simple and do not require an in-depth analysis of past behaviours or cognitions – the Constancies provide immediate guidance. One can begin to get FIT without the professional assistance of a clinical psychologist or therapist. In FIT, issues can also, in principle, be solved in an instant.

FIT and other personal development programmes

There are many books on personal development strategies, personal growth, positive thinking, and more effective self-management. Below we outline four examples. The first, stress management, is more an eclectic mix of information, advice and coping processes to deal with the demands of modern living. The second is an approach that is aimed particularly at the development of personal skills in a management context. The third is rooted in cognitive-behavioural therapy and has been applied to normal people to reduce their risks of stress and ill-health. The fourth is an example that has been very popular in the personal development field generally and has spawned many workshops, videos and other programmes.

Stress management

Whatever is meant by the term 'stress' probably includes some part of the term 'living'. To live is to be stressed at least some of the time. At some time in their lives everyone suffers some stress. Some people seem to be stressed a great deal. Some say they are never stressed and some of them die early or seem to be good at passing it to others. These are some of the reasons for including stress management courses in this chapter. These courses provide advice and guidance on how to live. Some of this should be useful to everyone if they are effective.

Stress management programmes are generally a mixture of sensible information and advice with initial training in some useful coping mechanisms and stress prophylactics. They can take many different forms but commonly include such things as:

- Information to show how widespread stress is, the common causes of strain, and the ways in which stress may be manifested in individuals. Many stress programmes are for managers, even though 'executive stress' is one of the bigger myths these programmes do not usually debunk. Information alone can be very helpful and some companies have employee advisory resources which focus on advice and referral information rather than counselling and personal help.

- An outline of different coping mechanisms and their likely efficacy (e.g. denial has little benefit; talking to others and getting support is very helpful). There may be role-play situations to give insights into how the different techniques feel to use.

- An introduction to personal stress-reduction techniques such as relaxation, yoga, meditation, often combined with lifestyle advice (including diet, alcohol intake, and smoking).

- Some programmes include explicit management training in areas that often cause problems for managers (perhaps also on topics such as dealing with harassment). Stress management courses often include sessions on time management and strategies to improve efficiency (such as dealing with paperwork once only, better delegation, getting the most out of others, etc.). Some programmes, usually those to improve leadership of teamwork, may involve an outdoor pursuits element too.

- An introduction to useful cognitive strategies that may reduce stress in the future, such as different types of positive thinking, seeing the issues from the other viewpoint, getting problems in perspective, being more assertive, or whatever.

- Basically, at best, stress management courses provide individuals a set of stress inoculation techniques that revolve around providing the individual with information, new constructive techniques, and the opportunity to model the learning in a non-threatening situation.

Stress management programmes and courses can be very useful. What little evaluation that has been done of their effectiveness is generally supportive. The evaluation is usually only done with the better ones and then it is usually impossible to say what elements of the multi-faceted course was beneficial. Many programmes the authors have seen have been poorly constructed and conceived, run by those with little expertise, and doubtless leave their participants with false ideas, and even harmful ones.

Although the better stress management programmes may be beneficial they do not provide long-term solutions. This is because they cannot tackle the primary causes of the stress itself. They are meant to provide the individual with a shield with which to deflect the core problems. Even when they assist in providing the person with useful techniques, these are often quite domain-specific (for work or one aspect of it, for example) and do not have more general value. FIT tries to provide a general tool that has direct relevance to the person and the way they deal with their environment in all aspects. Increasingly, companies provide organization-level programmes and interventions for work stress (e.g. Employee Advisory Programmes, Post-trauma staff counselling, work redesigns). Research by Dr Rob Briner and Professor Shirley Reynolds has shown that such initiatives are costly, but of little help, and sometimes harmful. This is consistent with the FIT framework – the individual needs to be the focus of change.

The seven habits of success

The second approach to personal development we will consider takes a management development slant, although there are many personal development programmes of this kind. Of the many thousands, perhaps one of the most influential and well known is Steven Covey's ideas on personal change encapsulated in his multi-million selling book *The Seven Habits of Highly Effective People* first published in 1989. Covey suggests ways in which individuals can improve their performance by developing a series of what he calls 'habits'. These he lists as:

Habit 1: Be Proactive – rather than responsive.

Habit 2: Begin With the End in Mind – have a clear goal.

Habit 3: Put First Things First – effective self-management in a time-efficient fashion.

Habit 4: Think Win/Win – most situations do not require one of the parties to lose in a transaction.

Habit 5: Seek First to Understand, Then Be Understood – seeing and understanding the other side.

Habit 6: Synergize – the sum benefits of co-operation are worth much more than the individuals could separately achieve.

Habit 7: Sharpen the Saw – to keep yourself in shape in all ways:
>Physically
>Mentally
>Social/Emotionally
>Spiritually

For Covey, progress in business and personal life is all about moving from a state of dependence (on others and other things) through independence or self-reliance (in financial, physical and psychological matters) to becoming interdependent (because all things in the world are related). Progress is about moving from You, to Me, to We. Covey provides guidelines for how the individual may do this, and how to recognize that it is happening.

All well and good, perhaps. But Covey does not offer any kind of integrated theory either to substantiate what he suggests or to provide the individual with more than exhortations about what might be useful. It is not a theory about the psychology of people, or the differences between them – it is a recipe for success. It is also probably flawed because it is rooted in the historical analysis of what has made people successful previously (as is, for example, Peters and Waterman's famous book *In Search of Excellence* which looked at the characteristics of [previously] successful companies). It offers no hope of personal integration, or inner sanctity, unless the sole criterion is outer success. FIT has a different perspective. It presumes outer success – the right internal states oblige that – but it also integrates this with a personal psychology and a theory about why people make the decisions they do and behave in the way they do. FIT is an integrated theory of how people actually do things. It has Inner Integrity. It balances external with internal success. Most management 'movements' emphasize either one or the other.

Creative Novation Therapy

A different kind of approach to personal development, and one which has been shown to have real personal benefits in the physical health sense, has been spearheaded by the world-renowned psychologist Professor Hans J. Eysenck and a practitioner Dr Grossarth-Maticek. This was first published in the *Journal of Behavioural Research and Therapy* in 1991. The approach is called Creative Novation Therapy (CNT). It has been developed from behavioural therapy, one of the cornerstones of modern psychological theory and clinical psychology. It involves people learning to create new behaviours that increase the likelihood of them experiencing positive feelings. This is done by a personal analysis of what produces positive and negative thoughts in the person's life.

The researchers have shown that CNT can dramatically reduce mortality from a whole range of killing diseases, including cancer and heart disease. For example, in long-term studies of initially healthy people they showed that people who participated in just a few hours of CNT reduced cancer and heart disease mortality manyfold up to 15 years later, spent fewer days in hospital over the years, and were more likely to benefit from traditional medical treatments. They have also shown that it does not require costly individual sessions with a professional to be beneficial: it can be done using bibliotherapy – or via written explanations with a minimum of professional backup. An outline of the framework of CNT is shown in Figure 9.2.

The benefits of CNT can be seen in terms of the changes in how people see their own role in determining what happens to them. The benefits of CNT also rest upon the individual being able to successfully jettison their past (and dysfunctional) behaviours and put in their place a new set of behaviours. This results in owning a set of behaviours that are more suitable for them internally. Unlike FIT, CNT does not require that these 'new' behaviours are linked to the situational requirements – the only need is for them to make the person feel better. Nonetheless, as in FIT, the person needs to become more aware of the link between their states and what they do, and to take more self-responsibility for this in such a way as to change their world and what happens to them. The FITness perspective offers a somewhat wider set of parameters of control than CNT but does require a similar framework of decision and behavioural analysis. CNT also shares with FIT the central idea that the individual needs to jettison past learning in order to progress.

Neuro-Linguistic Programming

There is a fourth category of personal development programme that has a broad approach to learning and change in which the individual is centre-stage. An example of this would be NLP or 'Neuro-Linguistic Programming', which was developed by John Grinder and Richard Bandler. NLP provides a framework for the development of practical skills that were derived from an analysis of the difference between the excellent and the ordinary. NLP forms the basis of other self-improvement approaches, including Anthony Robbins' programmes outlined in his books, tapes, videos and courses such as *Awaken the Giant Within* and *Unlimited Power*.

FIGURE 9.2 Core elements of Creative Novation Therapy (adapted from Eysenck and Grossarth-Maticek, 1991)

The basis of CNT is represented by the following ideas that together form the crux of personal behavioural change:

People can alter their behaviour to achieve an independent and healthy personality.

Behaviours can have consequences that are unpleasant, negative and harmful.

People can do one of three things in the face of unpleasant circumstances:

- change behaviour
- withdraw or avoid circumstances which make one unhappy
- change mental attitudes and values.

To change behaviour or attitudes one must:

- observe oneself carefully and identify:
    - the conditions which produce unpleasantness
    - what can be done to change the conditions
    - what new behaviours could be used in these conditions
- imagine new and alternative behaviours and try them out in mind and action
- remember that your own needs are important and not to always give precedence to others' needs.

Trial and error will need to be employed because success will take time and experience of failure as well as success.

A person should aim to produce autonomous self-activated behaviour to lead a happy life.

Replace behaviours that produce unhappiness with those that produce happiness.

Support and help of others will be useful and important.

Contentment through changed behaviours is achievable.

The four building blocks, or pillars, of NLP are 'rapport' (trust and responsiveness), 'goals' (knowing what you want), 'sensory acuity' (using your senses) and 'behavioural flexibility' (widening your choices). On the basis of these building blocks NLP purports to provide people with techniques to move them from the ordinary to the excellent. This learning takes them from stages of unconscious incompetence, through conscious incompetence and conscious competence, to unconscious competence. This last stage is when a person has developed the natural mastery of a new target skill. To get to that stage requires a deliberate and informed attempt to change from the unskilled level: most people do not attempt this. Like CNT, people have to be motivated to go through the effort and problems involved in creating a set of new and more appropriate behaviours which are necessary for change or mastery. Like CNT, the learning is also in the doing – in changing actual behaviours. In NLP people have to 'model' the new or desired behaviour both internally and externally and NLP provides a set of terminologies and techniques to facilitate this, such as 'matching' another's behaviour, 'anchoring' or associating something with the desired behaviour, or 'self-modelling' your own excellence in new situations.

Many of the writings of the NLP tradition attempt to demonstrate how imprisoned people are in their own 'map of reality' (which is not reality, but the schema they build up of their reality), how their senses or 'representational systems' bias how they see and learn, and how powerful psychological processes govern what we perceive and how we build and maintain our own maps. For example, in NLP terminology, we 'delete' or omit to see things that are not in accord with our maps, we 'distort' or change experiences to fit, and we 'generalize' without taking sufficient account of exceptions.

There are clear analogies between aspects of FIT and NLP. Perhaps the most obvious of these is the central role in both of awareness or conscious consideration of situations. This is a 'pillar' of NLP and the pre-eminent Constancy in FIT. Without it there is no change and no new learning. In both FIT and NLP this awareness is required at all levels, sensory to social evaluation. In FIT the primary model of the self is contained in the level of the individual's Constancy templates. In order to change, the individual needs to alter the level of their Constancy templates and act with greater Awareness, Fearlessness, Morality, Self-responsibility, and Balance considerations. In NLP the primary model of a person's self is their own 'map of reality'. In this regard, FIT presents a much simpler picture: if the Constancies are given greater primacy in decision making these will become more appropriate and behaviour FITter. The NLP 'map' is multi-level and complex and most of the NLP system is based around effecting changes in it through the large number of prescribed techniques. NLP really consists of a (useful) bag of techniques and not a theory about the structure of people, although it does make a number of general points, derived from a wealth of previous psychological research, about perception and learning.

In FIT the emphasis is on developing a behavioural repertoire to be able to behave appropriate to the situation, instead of having to fall back on old habits. Behavioural flexibility is also one of the central goals of

NLP since that is the way in which people can increase the number of their choices in any situation. In FIT, however, behavioural flexibility is partly dependent upon the state of the Constancy templates, whereas for NLP it is something to be worked on in its own right. NLP provides ideas about techniques that would increase flexibility. The difference in emphasis is key. In FIT theory the Constancies should provide the backbone for decisions and behaviours and, therefore, the real basis of appropriately enhanced behavioural flexibility. In NLP there is no such dependency: behavioural flexibility is simply useful.

Concluding Remarks

In this book we have attempted to provide a perspective on personal and organizational development that can really facilitate change. At an academic and theoretical level we believe this requires a reconsideration of some key psychological ideas and scientific methods. In some areas we believe it necessitates paradigm shifts and reconceptualizations. At the practical level we believe FIT has great potency and value. It is also our view that people and society need FIT, or something like it. Otherwise past ills will be recycled.

Do not let your future be your past continued. Reject a past perspective (which is ubiquitous and pernicious) and replace it with the present – for future's sake. If you want a different (better) future you need to intervene. The FIT framework may provide you with an appropriate personal intervention tool.

Glossary of terms

This glossary of terms provides a simple description of each of the key FITness terms or phrases. Reading the relevant parts of the text (see index) will provide further understanding. The list is initially arranged in decreasing levels of abstraction of the concepts, instead of alphabetically.

FITness, (Inner) FITness, or FIT

FIT is an acronym for 'flexible, innovative, trainable', or 'framework for internal transformation', or 'freedom from internalized torture'. A FIT person decides and behaves appropriately and with FIT Integrity.

unFITness

This is the opposite of FITness. The unFIT individual allows their past (including genes, natural dispositions and learned behaviours) to determine their choices and behaviours to a greater extent than is appropriate to the demands of the situation.

Appropriate decisions, behaviour and response

A FIT person behaves and decides what is appropriate to the context or situation. The less FIT an individual is the more likely they are to base decisions and behaviours on their natural pre-dispositions, habits, past learning and other context-independent factors. In other words, they are less likely to make appropriate or FIT decisions and to show appropriate behaviours. An appropriate decision, behaviour or response is something that an independent reasonable person would agree was best: it is something a really FIT person would decide or do.

Integral Person

An individual who manages to resist their past to a greater degree and does not react in an unFIT way to demands (i.e. is not imprisoned by their personal history, past learning, social pressures, work demands, needs and wants, parental pressures, genetic and other behavioural pre-dispositions etc.). An Integral Person is more likely to take heed of the FIT Constancies in their decisions and actions.

Well-heeded ideas

Many people say they know what they want, but are unsuccessful in achieving it to varying degrees. This is partly because they use fantasies or poorly thought out ideas and wants, instead of well-heeded ideas. These are well thought-out or thoroughly considered ideas, which have been subjected to proper consideration of needs and consequences and which also guide behaviours. This is why well-heeded ideas usually work out in reality – in a practical sense they could be considered as necessary bridges to personal and other goals becoming realized. A FIT individual is more likely to have well-heeded ideas. A FIT Corporation is more likely to operate according to well-heeded ideas.

The FIT Profiler™

This is a psychometric instrument that measures how FIT an individual is in terms of all the various FIT variables and scores. This book contains a short version of *The FIT Profiler™*.

Overall FITness score

This is a score derived from *The FIT Profiler™* and varies between 1 and 1000, where 1000 is very FIT. It is a global FIT score that takes account of both FIT Integrity and Behavioural Flexibility.

FITness EXERcises

These are a series of practical exercises, based upon the FITness framework, that may assist an individual to improve their FITness levels. Some short examples of these are included in this book in Chapter 6.

FIT Integrity

The degree to which an individual is Self-responsible, Fearless, Moral/ Ethical, Aware and maintains Balance (these are the five FIT 'Constancies'). In *The FIT Profiler™* the FIT Integrity score is expressed as a percentage.

Behavioural Flexibility or BFlex

People generally have a rather narrow range of behaviours (often described by the term 'personality') which means that in many situations they cannot act appropriately. Behavioural Flexibility is having the possibility of showing a wide range of behaviours should the context require it. For example, a FIT individual would be able to be introvert or extrovert, spontaneous or systematic, individually or group-centred, calm or energetic etceteras. In *The FIT Profiler*™, fifteen such behaviours are measured. The FIT person will show either pole or end of a 'personality trait' depending upon situational requirements, whereas many people are imprisoned by their personality to one end of the dimension. In *The FIT Profiler*™ the score for Behavioural Flexibility can be between 1 and 100, with 100 being the most flexible.

FITFlex score
This is a score derived from *The FIT Profiler*™, which shows the percentage of behavioural dimensions an individual shows of signs of FIT behaviour (where they exhibit behaviours on both sides of the mid-point of a behavioural dimension).

Polarity score
This is a score derived from *The FIT Profiler*™, which shows the percentage of the 15 behavioural dimensions on which an individual reports responses on only one side of the behavioural dimension. Polar behaviour suggests greater inflexibility.

Extremity score
This is a score derived from *The FIT Profiler*™. It is a more extreme scoring of 'Polarity' and reflects the percentage of the 15 behavioural dimensions on which an individual reports responses at only one extreme end (at least 4 or 5) of the behavioural dimension. A high extremity score would suggest inflexible behaviour.

Constancies
These are behavioural and cognitive templates that guide or inform FIT behaviour. They are constantly and continuously used to decide what to do, decide and choose. In the FIT framework there are five of them: Awareness, Fearlessness, Self-responsibility, Morality and Ethics, and Balance. In *The FIT Profiler*™ Constancy scores can vary between 1 and 10, with a higher score being FITter.

Awareness
This is one of the five Constancies and is the engine and constant monitor of FITness. Awareness or 'awakeness' is probably a basic requirement if a person is to develop their FITness. Awareness is the degree to which an individual monitors and attends to their internal and

external worlds. Many people have low awareness and can be said to 'sleep with their eyes open' most of the time.

Fearlessness

Fear plays a key role in decisions and behaviours for most people. Fearlessness is the emotional Constancy in FIT. Fearlessness is acting without fear or trepidation, or essentially facing the unknown with the same bravado as the known. Fear, contrary to popular and some theoretical positions, serves no useful purpose for the FIT individual. Fearlessness, on the other hand, aids appropriate decisions and responses.

Self-responsibility

Self-responsibility is one of the five Constancies. In many ways it is a key motivator and direction-giver because the extent to which an individual believes they can control what happens to them is a determinant of what they may try to achieve. Self-responsibility is the degree to which an individual accepts personal accountability for their world irrespective of the impact or role of factors outside themselves. In FIT, if a person takes responsibility for something then it is likely to happen. Most people, however, see themselves as victims in a vicarious universe that serves to constrain them – they fail to take sufficient Self-responsibility.

Balance

This is a Constancy which judges the emphasis that should be given to the different areas of life that should be balanced and manages their integration. Balance is making sure that each aspect of life receives due care and attention. The important parts should have a sufficient level of effort put into them and the person receive sufficient satisfaction from them. For most individuals three areas requiring balance are work; non-work or domestic, social and personal; and the self dimension.

Morality and Ethics

All decisions and behaviours should be guided by moral and ethical consideration. In FIT there is no absolute set of moral guidelines since these are not sufficiently situationally sensitive. However, a FIT individual will always make moral and ethical decisions and act in that way. The Morality/Ethics Constancy is the social conscience manager for FIT.

SCIchange

This is a scientific way of evaluating and promoting an emphasis on change. Traditionally science has advanced by investigating aspects of constancy and has developed, theories, models, techniques and methods to dissect the world. However, SCIchange suggests a slight change of emphasis in which change, not constancy, is the focus of the science. A SCIchange approach is more applicable than a 'traditional science' perspective to many practical issues, including personal and organizational development.

Stress or strain

This is not the same thing as 'demand' that many commentators assume. Stress may occur when the demands and constraints outweigh the supports that an individual has to cope with them. Thus, a high level job may be extremely demanding but will not be stressful if the person has few constraints or many supports to assist them. Strain is the negative outcomes that result from stress – for example, feeling anxious or depressed, or having low job satisfaction. Strains come in many guises from minor changes in physiology or behaviour, poor performance, bad interpersonal relationships, to disease and premature death. *The FIT Profiler*™ measures strain in the guise of general (or 'free floating') anxiety and depression.

Personality

This is the invariance in reactions and behaviours that individuals show across different circumstances. Personality can be considered as those aspects of a normal individual's decisions and behavioural pre-dispositions that are independent of the context or circumstance. In this sense, personality will result in inappropriate behaviours unless the context is within the persons normal comfort zone.

Comfort Zone (and Discomfort Zone)

The Comfort Zone is the range of behaviours and decisions an individual has an appropriate behavioural repertoire for and feels comfortable with. An inflexible person will have a smaller Comfort Zone than a flexible person. The Discomfort Zone is the range of acceptable and appropriate behaviours with which a person does not feel comfortable and for which they do not have an appropriate behavioural repertoire.

Feelings lag

This is the gap between trying out behaviours which are appropriate to the circumstance but which happen to be in your Discomfort Zone and feeling comfortable with them (when they become part of your Comfort Zone).

Culture (Organizational or Company)

This can be considered as the personality of the company or organization. It is the degree to which, or the way in which, companies and other collections of individuals are unresponsive in an appropriate manner (or responsive in an inappropriate way) to demands that require a response.

Polar Culture

Polar Culture is the term given to a work or organizational culture which has a characteristic way of responding to business, employee and other demands and requirements. Different Polar Cultures would describe more or less all organizations in one way or another, just as individuals can be said to have personalities. However, Polar Cultures are inflexible because they cannot respond appropriately when the organization needs to display the opposite end of the dimensions that characterizes them. For example, a bureaucratic organization may be unresponsive (or inappropriately responsive) to a creative idea from someone at the lowest level. Or a 'caring' company may not have sufficiently rigorous or hard-edged HR systems to cope with exploitative individuals. Polar Cultures may be relatively effective for some circumstances and business contexts, but they are likely to become less effective the more these contexts change.

The FIT Corporation™

A FIT Corporation is one in which the individuals that work in it are FIT. The FITter the individuals that are employed in the organization, the closer it comes to being a FIT Corporation. A FIT Corporation would also respond appropriately to the business and other demands under which it is placed. A FIT Corporation is a flexible organization that would move with the times and the changing demands.

References

Apter, M. (1997) *Reversal Theory: applications & developments*, Cardiff: University College Cardiff Press

Apter, M. (1997) Reversal theory: What is it? *The Psychologist*, May, 217–222

Blinkhorn, S. and Johnson, S. (1990) The insignificance of personality testing, *Nature*, 348, 20–27

Briner, R. and Reynolds, S. (1999) The costs, benefits, and limitations of organisational level stress interventions, *Journal of Organisational Behaviour*, 20(5), 647–64

Carver, C. S. and Schier, M. F. (1996) *Perspectives on personality*, 3rd ed., Allyn & Bacon

Cattell, R. (with Mason D. R.) (1976) *Handbook of modern personality theory*, Washington: Hemisphere Publishing Corporation

Cohen, S. & Taylor, L. (1992) *The Theory and Practice of Resistance to Everyday Life*, New York: Routledge

Covey, S. (1989) *The Seven Habits of Highly Effective People: Restoring the Character Ethic*, London: Simon & Schuster

Csikszentmihalyi, M. (1975) *Beyond boredom and anxiety: The experience of play in work and games*, Jossey-Bass

Csikszentmihalyi, M. and LeFevre, J. (1989) Optimal experience in work and leisure, *Journal of Personality and Social Psychology*, 5, 815–822

Epstein, S. (1994) Interaction of the cognitive and psychodynamic unconscious, *American Psychologist*, 49 (8), 709–724

Epstein, S. (1997) This I have learned from over 40 years of personality research, *Journal of Personality*, 65 (1), 3–33

Eysenck, H. J. (with Grossarth-Maticek, R.) (1991) Creative novation behaviour therapy as a prophylactic treatment for cancer and coronary heart disease, *Journal of Behavioural Research and Therapy*, 29 (1), 1–31

Eysenck, M. (1997) *Anxiety and Cognition*, Hove: Psychology Press

Fletcher, B. (C) (1991) *Work, Stress, Disease and Life Expectancy*, Chichester, UK: John Wiley

Fletcher, B. (C) (with Jones, F.) (1996) An empirical study of occupational stress transmission, *Human Relations*, 46, 881–903

Fletcher, B. (C) (with Jones, F.) (1996) Taking home work: A study of daily fluctuations in work stresses, effects on moods and impacts on marital partners, *Journal of Occupational and Organisational Psychology*, 69, 89–106

Frone, M. (1997) Relation of work-family conflict to health outcome: A four year longitudinal study of employed parents, *Journal of Occupational and Organisational Psychology*, 70, 325–335

Garfield, C. (1986) *Peak Performers: The New Heroes in American Business*, London: Hutchinson

Goleman, D. (1995) *Emotional intelligence: Why it can matter more than IQ*, Bloomsbury

Iso-Ahola, S. (1980) *The social psychology of leisure and recreation*, Dubuque, IA: William C. Brown

James, W. (1960) *Varieties of Religious Experience: a study in human nature*, London: Fontana

Kofodimus, J. (1993) *Balancing Act*, Jossey-Bass

Little, B. (with Ian McGregor) (1998) Personal projects, happiness and meaning: On doing well and being yourself, *Journal of Personality and Social Psychology*, 74 (2) 494–512

Maslow, A. (1954) *Motivation and Personality*, New York: Harper & Row

Oates, W. (1971) *Confessions of a Workaholic: the facts about work addiction*, London: Wolfe

Parikh, J. (1991) *Managing Your Self: Management by Detached Involvement*, Blackwell

Peters, T. J. and Waterman, R. H. (1982) *In Search of Excellence: Lessons from America's Best-run Companies*, New York: Harper & Row

Rachman, S. (1974) *The Meanings of Fear*, Harmondsworth: Penguin

Rotter, J. (1966) Generalised expectancies for internal versus external control of reinforcement, *Psychological Monographs*, 80 (1), Whole 609

Rowe, B. (1987) *Beyond fear*, Fontana

Snyder, M. (1987) *Public Appearances/Private Realities*, New York: W. H. Freeman & Co

Stacey, R. (1992) *Managing chaos: dynamic business strategies in an unpredictable world*, London: Kogan Press

Verstraeten, J. (1998) From business ethics to the vocation of business leaders to humanise the world of business, *A European Review*, 7 (2), 111–124

Index